From Mind to Heart

From Mind to Heart

Christian Meditation Today

Peter Toon

BAKER BOOK HOUSE
Grand Rapids, Michigan 49516

Copyright 1987 by
Baker Book House Company

Printed in the United States of America

Library of Congress Cataloging-in-Publication Data

Toon, Peter, 1939-
    From mind to heart.
    1. Meditation.   I. Title.
BV4813.T66   1987   248.3'4   87-19607
ISBN 0-8010-8887-9

For **Eileen Johnson,**
faithful deaconess
of the church in Boxford

Contents

Part 2   Examples of Method

Preface

I have written this book to encourage fellow Christians to join me in responding to the call of God through the apostle James, who wrote, "Come near to God and he will come near to you" (4:8). Please do not think that I see myself as an expert. Far from it! I see myself as your fellow pilgrim, seeking to walk to God, in, through, and with the Lord Jesus. In this book I invite you to share insights I have gained from Christians who have walked before us in the highway of holiness, who have sat in the school of prayer and have meditated upon God's Word by day and by night.

In particular, I have had in mind as I write two kinds of fellow believers. On the one hand, I offer a word of advice to those in college or seminary who desire to know God more intimately in personal and corporate prayer and worship. On the other hand, I give a word of encouragement to older Christians who recognize that their interior lives need to be revitalized or reordered. This book should be viewed as a personal letter from one pilgrim to other pilgrims, one soldier to other soldiers, and one disciple to other disciples. I request simply that you accompany me in discovering (or rediscovering) the practice of the art of meditation, as a way provided by God both into prayerful communion with himself and into deeper commitment to his perfect will.

By *meditation* I mean that meditation which has been practiced within the Christian church over the centuries and which has been described in detail by a host of writers, both Catholic and Protestant. This practice itself is commanded in the Bible. After Moses had died God directed Joshua, "Do not let this Book of the Law depart from your mouth; *meditate* on it day and night, so that you may be careful to do everything written in it" (Josh. 1:8, italics mine). Meditation is thus a particular way of receiving the revealed and dynamic Word of God into the heart from the mind so as to direct the will in the way of God's guidance. It is related to, but not identical with, intellectual Bible study and prayer.

This biblical approach to meditation must not be confused with the Eastern method of seeking interior silence, which is also called meditation. The Eastern aim of achieving pure awareness without thought and of experiencing mystical consciousness is the basic task of meditation groups. Many participants also believe that this Eastern style of meditation improves physical and mental health and relieves stress. And it often does—if for no other reason than the techniques bring relaxation throughout the whole body.

Practitioners of Eastern methods commonly deny that meditation ever includes "thinking about something." In contrast, Christian meditation always begins (but never ends) with thinking about something—namely, the revealed Word of God. Both methods, however, recognize the importance of daily discipline and also of right bodily posture. Keeping trunk, spine, neck, and head in an upright line is a way of maintaining poised wakefulness and concentration.

In the meditation of the East, individuals are in search of their true self; in the meditation of the West, individuals are in search of their true Maker, the God and Father of our Lord Jesus Christ. Thus, in spite of similarities in methods and psychosomatic benefits, the respective aims are very different. A Western Christian may indeed learn from the meditation of the Buddhist or Hindu, especially in terms of bodily posture, discipline, and commitment. Some Christians claim also to have learned about prayer, mystical experience, and contemplation. I take these claims with some reserve, simply because biblical meditation always starts with the revealed Word of God and the employment of the mind in considering that Word. The meditation may lead on, by the inspiration of the Holy Spirit, to a mystical experience of God, but it is a God as Lord, who is Creator, Redeemer, and Judge, as well as he who, by the Spirit, dwells in the human soul. The true God is thus both transcendent and immanent. For those who want to study Eastern methods, there is an abundant literature. As a starter I recommend James Hewitt, *Teach Yourself Meditation* [London: Hodder and Stoughton, 5th ed., 1986], which looks at the most important Eastern traditions of meditation.

In this book I refer only occasionally to these Eastern methods. In part 1 we examine the Bible's own comments about meditation. We shall find that the message of both Old and New Testament, of Jesus and his apostles, is that meditation is a necessary part of what we today call spirituality. Then in part 2 we shall look at a variety of Western Christian approaches to, and methods of meditation in order to encourage one another to adopt one of these and to begin practicing the (Western) method of meditation—and to do so in order to please our Lord Jesus Christ! This is the only *sound* reason.

Advent 1986   Peter Toon

Introduction: Why Meditate?

In our heart of hearts, we recognize that a duty must be good and wholesome for us if the Lord himself has urged it upon us. Such is the case with meditation, as we shall see in chapters 2–4. Yet, as beginners in the school of Jesus, we do like to be assured that, if we are to engage in a particular discipline, it will ultimately, and preferably sooner, have observable, positive results. This is especially the case when we suspect (quite rightly concerning meditation) that we are being asked to engage in a demanding spiritual exercise.

I thus list here the kinds of benefits and blessings which our Lord *normally* causes to be experienced by those who prayerfully meditate each day upon his Word in reliance upon his Spirit. In doing so, however, I must emphasize that in spiritual growth (according to the witness of the Bible and the saints before us) there will be periods of dryness and aridity of soul when we must continue with our discipline even though we do not feel like it and benefits are hard to discern. We believe, trust, obey, meditate, and pray because there is love for our Lord in our hearts and because we know that there is no other way but the way of persevering through good times and bad, over hill and through valley.

1. *Meditation can bring sanity and balance into our activism.* The tendency of healthy Westerners is always to

be busy, often rushing and usually not having enough
time for all we want to do. Many Christians compress
their devotions into the minimum time—the short "Quiet
time" where "a little talk with Jesus makes it right,
alright."

For a mother with infant children, for example, making
the space and time for meditation/prayer is difficult: such
people have to learn to pray when they are doing basic,
repetitive jobs or lying in bed. Most of us will admit, however (if we are honest), that we do have space and time
to spend much longer in our devotions with our Lord than
we do in fact do. It is really a matter of making adjustments to our timetable and priorities so that spiritual
duty comes before other, less necessary activity. Of course,
there is no special virtue in taking a long time to pray;
we cannot truly meditate and pray, however, in less than
twenty minutes.

Time spent in meditation/prayer not only keeps the
muscles of our souls in good shape, so that we are open
to God and the prompting of his Spirit through his Word;
it can also have a beneficial effect physically and psycho-
logically. A time of stillness and silence in the Lord's presence is truly recreation (also re-creation) and relaxation.
Those who use methods of meditation from the East or
from the Eastern churches claim to experience the following phenomena: the heart rate decreases by two or three
beats a minute, the rate of breathing also decreases, the
body's consumption of oxygen decreases by up to 20 per-
cent (much the same as happens in sleep), blood lactate
decreases (thus reducing anxiety), high blood pressure goes
down, and the brain produces alpha and perhaps theta
waves (which indicate relaxation). Much the same can
happen to those using the Western methods I describe in
part 2 of this book, especially as meditation becomes or
leads into contemplative prayer.

Let us be honest with ourselves. We are often on the
move: we need to be still. We are bombarded with a con-

stant cacophony of noise: we need to be silent. We are subject to a constantly changing barrage of images and propaganda from the media: we need to have time to receive and digest the images and truth of God's holy Word. And we are enclosed by a landscape increasingly dominated by the results of scientific and technological advances, designed to make our lives more comfortable: we need also to gaze upon God in the face of Jesus Christ our Lord. Prayer, meditation, and contemplation are necessary—if only to bring balance to our lives.

2. *The Scriptures are the faithful written record of God's self-disclosure to human beings; meditation enables us to begin to use them for the purpose God intended.* What Paul claimed for the Hebrew Scriptures is also true of the Christian Bible: "All Scripture is God-breathed and is useful for teaching, rebuking, correcting and training in righteousness, so that the man of God may be thoroughly equipped for every good work" (2 Tim. 3:16–17). In order to be a faithful spokesperson for his Lord, the preacher and teacher must not only study the Scriptures but also meditate upon them. Likewise, in order to be a faithful disciple of Jesus, each Christian must both study the sacred text and also meditate upon it.

Meditation does not eliminate reverent study. Certainly the church as a whole needs experts to translate the Scriptures into our modern languages, to provide commentaries on the books of the Bible, to prepare concordances, lexicons, and dictionaries, and generally to help us all gain a better appreciation of the context of the Bible and what it meant for its original readers and hearers. We ought to be grateful to God for all accurate, readable, and reverent scholarship, which aids our own study of the Word of God today.

We do not meditate in order to benefit from this kind of scholarship. Meditation is not catching up on the latest good exposition of a given book of the Bible. Meditation, as it were, sits on the shoulders of faithful and reverent study. When we study, our aim is to understand a given topic and to gain information about certain subjects. In study we often feel our hearts warmed, even though our aim has been to gain intellectual clarity, to inform our understanding, and to master a given topic. This benefit occurs because we are psychosomatic unities and our heart is not totally separated from our mind! It also happens because we are experiencing knowledge in two senses— first as rational information and second (in the Hebrew sense) as a sense of spiritual unity with God (see John 17:3).

Meditation is, at least to a certain extent, dependent upon reverent study, but it has a different function than study does. We meditate for much the same reason that we listen to a sermon, namely, to receive and digest the Word of God, spoken to us by the Lord Jesus in and through the Holy Spirit, using the sacred text. Our Lord Jesus wants us, as his disciples, truly to know God in spiritual fellowship and communion and thus to be walking in the way of godliness and holiness. In meditation, the Spirit can use the very text which he originally inspired to be written. He uses it to speak Christ's word to us as we consider it, reflect upon it, and ask how it bears upon our lives. We may thus say that study brings us the possibility of receiving God's Word as the living Word of God for today; meditation, then, supplies the actual opportunity and means to receive the dynamic, holy Word into our inmost beings and to work through our hearts and wills.

Meditation, like a cow's chewing her cud, is the way of inwardly digesting the Word of God. Study, we may say, is like the cow's initial eating of the grass. If the cow originally eats good grass, then the chewing of the cud will be an enjoyable and profitable experience.

3. *Meditation is one important way in which we open ourselves to God in order that the Holy Spirit may illuminate, energize, and guide us.* We believe, teach, and confess that our Lord Jesus Christ is exalted into heaven and there

is seated at the right hand of the Father in glory. Not only is he the King of Kings and Lord of Lords, but he is also the Head and Lifegiver of the church of God, which is his body. The dynamic personal link between the exalted Lord Jesus and ourselves, as members of his body, is the Holy Spirit, whom we rightly call the Spirit of Christ.

The Holy Spirit communicates to faithful believers that which the Lord Jesus wants them to receive, believe, and obey. Although the Holy Spirit sometimes uses extraordinary means (e.g., a "word of wisdom," "gift of prophecy," or "word of knowledge") to bring Christ's Word to his disciples, his normal way is that of gently and gradually illuminating the minds of believers in order that they see, as they meditate upon the sacred Scriptures, the message there is for them from heaven. And this ongoing process is confirmed and strengthened by the preaching and teaching within the church.

Meditation as a spiritual discipline is something that you and I actually do—we are quiet and still, we recall, we consider, we reflect, and so on. "To meditate" is an active, not passive, verb! In and through our activity, however, the Holy Spirit invisibly and secretly acts to illuminate our minds so that we see in Scripture the actual Word of God for us: he also stimulates our hearts so that we begin to desire and long for that which we have been told is good for us. Meditation is thus one aspect of the Christian life in which Paul's word is relevant: "Continue to work out your salvation with fear and trembling, for it is God who works in you to will and to act according to his good purpose" (Phil. 2:12–13).

4. *Meditation is an admirable and often necessary preparation for prayer and worship.* Certainly we can pray to the Lord and worship him without previously meditating upon his Word. Saints over the centuries, however, have observed that our prayer and worship is likely to be more truly "in spirit and in truth" if they follow meditation. Genuine meditation usually has the effect of raising our

spirits and desires and of causing us to want to adore, worship, and praise the Lord—or, as the case may be, to pour out our guilt before him and seek his forgiveness and grace.

Probably we could all agree that one natural and expected fruit of meditation is prayer; in fact, the dividing line between genuine meditation and sincere prayer is impossible to draw. As the heart is warmed through consideration of the Word of God, so it cannot but pray, and having prayed, it returns for more stimulation and encouragement to the Word. Furthermore, the spiritual quality of our public and corporate worship would be enhanced if, before it began, we engaged in quiet meditation before the Lord, looking to him to prepare us for spiritual worship. Then in times of quiet in services (e.g., in the administration of the bread and wine in Holy Communion), our receptivity to the grace of God will be enhanced by meditation.

5. *Meditation has the effect of motivating our will and desires to be as God wants us to be.* Good preaching has the effect of telling us what we ought to be doing for our Lord. In a similar way God uses meditation to instruct our consciences and direct our wills toward being and doing what is pleasing to him. Through meditation God not merely directs us but so raises our desires that we actually want, above all else, to be and do what he wants us to be and do. In meditation a channel is somehow opened between the mind, heart, and will—what the mind receives enters the heart and goes into action via the will. A matter that is at first considered is then desired and longed for and finally is prayed for or worked for.

Consider victory over a particular temptation. In reflecting on the Word of God, I see that it is wrong, for example, to chatter before a service of worship and that it is right to be prayerful and meditative. Furthermore, I feel that I want to give up my habit of talking until the first hymn is announced and that instead I want to seek to prepare myself for such a high calling as worshiping the almighty God. Finally I resolve that I shall do what is right in this matter, beginning at the first opportunity afforded me.

If we engage in meditation daily, it thus becomes an important channel by which we are being changed inwardly and outwardly according to the will of God. Of course, the process of turning away from sinfulness toward the beauty and perfection of God is never ending in this life; but the more we turn, the better is the glorious view we have of God in his holiness, glory, and excellence.

6. *Meditation is necessary in order to live a truly Christian life characterized by growth in holiness and love and by overcoming evil and sin.* Food kept cold in the refrigerator, cooking in the oven, or attractively placed on the dining table will not supply energy to our bodies unless we actually eat, chew, and digest it so that it passes into our bodies. As we have seen, meditation is like the process of digestion, for by it we take divine food into our souls.

The apostle Paul pictures Christians as soldiers in the army of the Lord Jesus, engaged in battle against the forces of evil and sin in God's world. He sees them as putting on the whole armor of God, including the belt of truth, the breastplate of righteousness, the shield of faith, and the helmet of salvation (Eph. 6:10–17). It takes time to get dressed, just as it took time for a Roman soldier to put on his whole battle gear. In meditation we actually begin to put on the whole armor of God to fight in Christ's battle. We must remember that this process of putting on the armor is not done in a minute—it takes time, and of course it must be repeated before each battle.

If we do not digest our food properly, we get indigestion, and we also lose the potential energy from the food. If we do not put on our whole armor, then we are easily injured in battle. There are no short cuts to true healthy digestion, and there is no simplified quick way of putting on the whole armor. Meditation is important, but it likewise takes time. In the next three chapters we shall see how men of both the old and new covenants, including our Lord himself, made time to meditate, and we shall notice that it was time well spent.

A prayer

Blessed Lord, who hast caused all holy Scriptures to be written for our learning: Grant that we may in such wise hear them, read, mark, learn and inwardly digest them, that by patience and comfort of thy holy Word, we may embrace and ever hold fast the blessed hope of everlasting life, which thou hast given us in our Saviour Jesus Christ. [For Advent 2, *Book of Common Prayer*]

PART **1**

The Biblical Way

1

Under the Old Covenant

Hebrew concordances and lexicons reveal that the verb "to meditate" (Heb. *hagah* and *siyach*) is not common: there are only about twenty examples in the Old Testament. The classic one outside the Psalter is contained in the Lord's command to Joshua: "Meditate on [the Book of the Law] day and night, so that you may be careful to do everything written in it" (Josh. 1:8). Here we get the important connection between God's revelation (law, or torah), meditation, and faithful obedience to God.

Psalm 119, which is a celebration of God's revelation in the torah, highlights meditation in a variety of ways. "I meditate on your precepts and consider your ways" (v. 15); "your servant will meditate on your decrees" (v. 23); "I will meditate on your precepts" (v. 78); and "my eyes stay open through the watches of the night, that I may meditate on your promises" (v. 148). Here again meditation points to the activity of reflecting upon and considering part or all of God's written Word (torah), with a view to being his true worshiper, servant, and covenant partner.

We shall look carefully below at four psalms whose contents give us important insights into the nature of meditation. First, however, we need to notice the use of the important verb "to remember" (Heb. *zakar*). It occurs as a form of command from God throughout the Book of

Deuteronomy in the style, "*Remember* what I, the LORD, have said to you and done for you." Then, in contrast, it is used in prayer addressed to the Lord by Israelites who call upon him to *remember* his choice of Israel and the covenant he made with his people. As they pray to God to remember, they expect to experience his presence and witness his power with and around them. God's act of making himself known to them can then be described as his remembering them.

The prophets, whose task it was to proclaim the Word of the Lord to the people, whether they wanted to hear or not, often called upon them *to remember* his mighty deeds, the conditions of the covenant made at Mount Sinai through Moses, and the blessings and judgments attached to that covenant. We may reflect that, had they done this remembering, they would have been saved from all kinds of faithlessness, backsliding, idolatry, wickedness, and unrighteousness.

Thus it is not surprising that in some contexts *I remember* refers to the prayerful activity before God of recalling what he has revealed to and done for Israel, with the aim of considering the implications for the present (e.g., Ps. 63:6; 137:6). Certainly this sense of the command to remember occurs in Deuteronomy. This command was addressed to the whole people and in particular to the head of each household. Each Sabbath, for example, was a time for remembering: "*Remember* that you were slaves in Egypt and that the LORD your God brought you out of there. . . . Therefore the LORD your God has commanded you to observe the Sabbath day" (5:15, italics mine). Each Saturday they were to meditate on the story of the exodus, using their imagination to picture its details in order to remind them of, and give them a desire to, observe their covenant with God.

Using the understanding, memory, and imagination in meditation was more than a once-weekly duty. It was to be a daily exercise, as Deuteronomy 11:18–21 makes clear.

Fix these words of mine in your hearts and minds; tie them as symbols on your hands and bind them on your foreheads. Teach them to your children, talking about them when you sit at home and when you walk along the road, when you lie down and when you get up. Write them on the doorframes of your houses and on your gates, so that your days and the days of your children may be many in the land that the LORD swore to give to your forefathers.

The commandments that God gave to Israel through Moses at Sinai provided the framework within which they were to express their love to him. Thus the law was to be on their hearts so that they often thought about it, meditated on its contents, and prayed to its holy Giver. By reflecting upon God's commandments and by understanding the manner of life required by the law, they were discovering the way in which they were to respond practically to God's love for them. They were to love him by doing what pleased him. Furthermore, having understood and spiritually digested the law, they were to pass it on to their children (see also Deut. 6:6–9). The route of God's revelation was thus from torah to the understanding, from the understanding to the heart, from the heart to the will, and from the will into action. Meditation had an important place in this divine chain.

Psalm 1

The First Psalm was written as an introduction to the whole Psalter. Among other things, it emphasizes that the practice of meditation is something which the godly habitually do.

> Blessed is the man
>   who does not walk in the counsel of the wicked
> or stand in the way of sinners
>   or sit in the seat of mockers.

> But his delight is in the law of the LORD,
> and on his law he meditates day and night.
> He is like a tree planted by streams of water,
>   which yields its fruit in season
> and whose leaf does not wither.
>   Whatever he does prospers.
>
> [vv. 1–3]

Here we learn that the truly happy person is one who does not conform to any principles or values which are contrary to God's revealed will. He or she does not accept the advice of, publicly identify with, or adopt in part or whole, the attitudes of those who reject God's Word.

The happiness of such persons consists in their conforming to God's will and delighting in God's written Word in the tôrah. In fact, they reflect upon its contents, consider them, imagine the joy of salvation experienced by their forefathers, and memorize them in order to know God's will for their own lives. They know that God commanded Joshua to engage in such meditation (Josh. 1:8) and that every true Israelite ought also to do the same every day of his or her life. To be a Jew, we may recall, is to live to the praise of God.

The benefits of delighting in and meditating upon God's written Word in the torah are conveyed through the picture of the fruitful tree which absorbs the water and then produces appetizing fruit. In a similar manner faithful believers absorb the Word of God (which is the water of life) into their souls in order to produce the genuine fruit of godliness.

Psalm 19

The Lord revealed himself in word and deed to Israel. He also made known his deity through the universe which he created by his Word and which he sustains by his almighty power. In the Nineteenth Psalm, King David supplies us with the substance of his meditation upon both sources of God's self-disclosure—upon the skies and the Scriptures. He had offered these thoughts to God:

> May the words of my mouth and the meditation of my
>   heart
>   be pleasing in your sight,
>   O LORD, my Rock and my Redeemer.
>
>   [v. 14]

David obviously believed that meditation was practiced in the presence of God and offered to him as mental prayer.

The first half of the psalm has been called a meditation upon the soundless music of the heavens.

> The heavens declare the glory of God;
>   the skies proclaim the work of his hands.
> Day after day they pour forth speech;
>   night after night they display knowledge.
> There is no speech or language
>   where their voice is not heard.
> Their voice goes out into all the earth,
>   their words to the ends of the world.
>
>   [vv. 1–4]

David felt that the vast expanse of the skies is constantly proclaiming, confessing, and celebrating the glory, excellence, and majesty of God—and doing so without uttering a word.

Perhaps the best way to comment on poetry is through poetry. Here is the poetic meditation of Joseph Addison (1672–1719) in his once-famous hymn, "The Spacious Firmament on High."

> [1] The spacious firmament on high,
>   With all the blue ethereal sky,
>   And spangled heavens, a shining frame,
>   Their great Original proclaim.

The unwearied sun, from day to day,
Doth his Creator's power display;
And publishes to every land
The work of an almighty hand.

2 Soon as the evening shades prevail,
The moon takes up the wondrous tale,
And nightly to the listening earth
Repeats the story of her birth:
Whilst all the stars that round her burn,
And all the planets in their turn,
Confirm the tidings as they roll,
And spread the truth from pole to pole.

3 What though in solemn silence all
Move round this dark terrestrial ball;
What though no real voice or sound
Amidst their radiant orbs be found:
In reason's ear they all rejoice,
And utter forth a glorious voice,
For ever singing as they shine,
"The hand that made us is divine."

Regrettably, we may think, "God's invisible qualities—
his eternal power and divine nature" (Rom. 1:20) revealed
in and through the created order are rarely consciously
perceived by Westerners today.

The second part of Psalm 19 contains a meditation on
the written Word of God, the torah.

The law of the LORD is perfect,
    reviving the soul.
The statutes of the LORD are trustworthy,
    making wise the simple.
The precepts of the LORD are right,
    giving joy to the heart.
The commands of the LORD are radiant,
    giving light to the eyes.
The fear of the LORD is pure,
    enduring forever.
The ordinances of the LORD are sure
    and altogether righteous.

> They are more precious than gold,
>   than much fine gold;
> they are sweeter than honey,
>   than honey from the comb.
> By them is your servant warned;
>   in keeping them there is great reward.
>
>   [vv. 7–11]

The revelation of the Lord not only regenerates, renews, and refreshes the receiver, it also makes the person wise.

The torah includes a variety of literary forms (narrative, statutes, precepts, ordinances, etc.); each one in particular and all together reveal the character and will of the God who entered into covenant with Israel. They are right, sure, pure, and clean, in perfect order to be received and obeyed. (Psalm 119 develops this theme in detail and depth.)

Meditation of this kind and in this way soon leads believers to value God's revelation highly, for they encounter the Divinity through the Hebrew words. They see the torah as more valuable than all the gold in the world and sweeter than the sweetest food known to them—honey fresh from the honeycomb.

David recognizes, however, that God's holy law is not merely to be admired as the creation of an almighty hand; it is also to be obeyed in order to express love for God and to glorify his name. Such obedience and love require the examination of conscience. When this is done there comes this recognition and prayer:

> Who can discern his errors?
>   Forgive my hidden faults.
> Keep your servant also from willful sins;
>   may they not rule over me.
> Then will I be blameless,
>   innocent of great transgression.
>
>   [vv. 12–13]

David found that meditation and prayer belong together
and that to admire God can cause a believer to see his or
her own sins in a new light.

Psalm 63

Meditation need not be within the enclosed walls of
palace or sanctuary. David offered the prayer of Psalm 63
to God in the wilderness, east of the river Jordan, when
he fled from Jerusalem to escape the wrath of Absalom
(see 2 Sam. 15:13–37).

> O God, you are my God,
>   earnestly I seek you;
> my soul thirsts for you,
>   my body longs for you,
>   in a dry and weary land
>   where there is no water.
>
> [v. 1]

The night was long in the deserted, rocky terrain, and so
he took the opportunity to recall God's promises to him
(see 2 Sam. 7:5–16).

> On my bed I remember you;
>   I think of you through the watches of the night.
> Because you are my help,
>   I sing in the shadow of your wings.
> My soul clings to you;
>   your right hand upholds me.
>
> [vv. 6–8]

We see here that meditation on God's promises leads to
increase in faith, closer fellowship, and deeper confidence
in God. Having begun to recollect the goodness of God
toward him and his people, David cannot turn his mind
to anything else. In fact he has to rejoice aloud when he

realizes not only that he is wholly dependent upon the Lord but that the Lord is wholly faithful toward him.

Psalm 77

Not all meditation begins in happy circumstances. Asaph had a problem which led him into urgent prayer. But he could not find peace in his repeated imploring of God.

> I cried out to God for help;
>   I cried out to God to hear me.
> When I was in distress, I sought the Lord;
>   at night I stretched out untiring hands
>   and my soul refused to be comforted.
>
> [vv. 1–2]

So he turned from searching and supplication to reflection and meditation, but this did not immediately help.

> I remembered you, O God, and I groaned;
>   I mused, and my spirit grew faint.
>
> [v. 3]

And the musing became somewhat negative and depressive.

> Will the Lord reject forever?
>   Will he never show his favor again?
> Has his unfailing love vanished forever?
>   Has his promise failed for all time?
> Has God forgotten to be merciful?
>   Has he in anger witheld his compassion?
>
> [vv. 7–9]

Such feelings have been experienced by believers under the new covenant as well as under the old. They have felt that a dark cloud separates them from their Lord. The psalmist's list is overwhelming and fearful; the Hebrew verbs are sharp and piercing. He goes beyond asking Why does not God do something? to the more perplexing question of whether, in fact, God *can* do anything. Such is the aridity of his heart and soul and his sense of separation from the Lord.

Yet this psalmist persevered and continued to talk to himself and to make himself begin to remember, recall, and repeat the mighty acts of God which were performed for his own people, the covenant people of Israel. As he thus considered with memory, understanding, and imagination, he came to this point:

> Then I thought, "To this I will appeal:
>   the years of the right hand of the Most High."
> I will remember the deeds of the LORD;
>   yes, I will remember your miracles of long ago.
> I will meditate on all your works
>   and consider all your mighty deeds.
>
>   [vv. 10–12]

This effort to talk to himself and to recall what God had done for, and was to, Israel had its eventual reward, as verse 13 testifies.

> Your ways, O God, are holy
>   What god is so great as our God?

We see here how memory—the storehouse of God's Word and deeds—is a most valuable capacity of the mind and can be used beneficially to begin and facilitate meditation.

The psalmist recalled what he had been taught from childhood at each Passover festival—the story of the exodus from Egypt via Sinai to the land of Canaan. We may say that he obeyed the command to remember, and using all powers of understanding and imagination, he did so—

and it worked. What began as a personal lament, leading to his questioning of the integrity of God as Lord, ends in a positive meditation and celebration of the faithful words and mighty works of the Lord.

The Book of Psalms is a textbook not only of prayer but also of meditation. If there were no other books available, we could learn the basic art and method as well as the right content of meditation, simply by noting how the psalmists went about this discipline in the context of service of the Lord.

Meditation is always on God's revelation of his deity and will. Certainly in meditation and prayer there is the need to be still, to be quiet, and to watch in order to recollect and become aware of the presence of God. However, the purpose of achieving quietness of soul and stillness of spirit before God is not to look within to discover God there or to find one's true self (as in Eastern meditation). Rather, the aim is to be open to the power and efficacy of the Word of God received in the mind, heart, and will.

Twice in Psalm 62 we encounter this confession:

> Truly my heart waits silently for God;
> my deliverance comes from him.
>
> [vv. 1, 5 NEB]

This silence comes from having said all and not knowing what else to say. But there is also the silence of adoration, of being lost for adequate words by which to praise God in the beauty of his holiness. This silence is expressed in the opening verse of Psalm 65, which in a fairly literal translation can be rendered, "There shall be silence before thee and praise, O God, in Zion."

The psalmists placed great emphasis on recalling from memory what they had learned concerning God's revelation in deeds and words (see Deut. 11:18–21) in order to consider it afresh in the understanding. Such recalling naturally involved the use of the imagination as the best means of bringing home to themselves the reality of that past experience of their forefathers.

They also made use of what we may call the soliloquy, a form of addressing oneself (especially when down-hearted, depressed, and overwhelmed) with positive questions and thoughts, as well as addressing God himself. We encountered this method in Psalm 77. Here we find it in Psalms 42:5, 11 and 43:5.

> Why are you downcast, O my soul?
> Why so disturbed within me?
> Put your hope in God,
> for I will yet praise him,
> my Savior and my God.

We shall see that this method of addressing oneself was favored by the Puritan writers on meditation.

2

The Example of Jesus

Jesus certainly meditated. How could he do otherwise when the classic portrait of the godly and righteous person in the Hebrew Scriptures includes meditation day and night upon God's law!

Yet the modern, Western reader of the four Gospels does not see any obvious references to Jesus actually involved in meditating. Nowhere in any translation of the Greek New Testament do we read, "and Jesus meditated." We do read that Jesus prayed often and was deeply versed in the sacred Scriptures. The Gospel of Luke presents Jesus at prayer before all the major events of his ministry, whereby we understand that he was constantly praying. And in the Sermon on the Mount recorded in Matthew 5–7, Jesus expressed his knowledge and commitment to sacred Scripture in his claim that he had come not to destroy but rather to fulfil (fill out the meaning of) the Law and the Prophets. In the light of such information we are to understand that Jesus' meditation arose from his reading and remembering the contents of the Scriptures and that this meditation was an important ingredient in his life of prayer and communion with his heavenly Father.

Jesus' Practice of Meditation

The place of meditation in Jesus' spiritual life may be illustrated by looking at his experience in the wilderness

35

of Judea after his baptism, in Caesarea Philippi with his
disciples, and in the Garden of Gethsemane just before
his trial and crucifixion.

In the Wilderness

The Gospels of Matthew and Luke provide us with descriptions of a profound, long, and necessary experience
of Jesus before he began his public ministry in Galilee
and Judea (Matt. 4 and Luke 4). We usually call this experience his temptation, and so it was, but much more
was going on in the loneliness of the barren wilderness
near the river Jordan. Traditionally we picture Jesus
calmly refusing to submit to Satanic temptation to become a popular Messiah who would be successful through
miraculous feeding of the hungry, spectacular stunts, and
compromise with the world.

However, there are other ways of approaching the accounts of the wilderness experience. Let us think of Jesus
as carefully going over in his mind the history of his
ancestors (i.e., recalling from memory the contents of the
book of Moses), whom we call Hebrews and Israelites,
especially their exodus from Egypt to Canaan, from misery to the Promised Land. We see him recalling this history both to understand what God had actually revealed
through Moses to Israel and to respond to that revealed
word in the right way. He seeks to determine what God
did for, said to, and desired of ancient Israel as well as to
see where Israel had failed in its response to the Lord.

In particular, the three temptations show that Jesus
was *meditating* on and considering this sacred history and
that Jesus himself (in his vocation as the new Israel, the
representative Messiah) was facing similar temptations
which his ancestors, God's covenant people, were not able
or willing to resist. In fact, the material contained in Luke 4
and Matthew 4 concerning the testing of Jesus is a com-
pressed account of what could be told in a long book.
Much more of what went on in his mind, heart, and will

as he sought to clarify his calling and task as Messiah could have been shared by Jesus, and so chosen. We have been given sufficient to see the nature (but not the details) of his profound experience.

We may imagine that, as he recalls the story of the exodus, he also receives into his mind and heart that self-revelation of God originally given to his ancestors. And having received and appropriated that revelation of God's character and will, he has to face the testing that they faced. As the new Israel he must recapitulate their testing and their temptations in order to come through victorious as the One who trusts, obeys, and loves the Lord, the God of the covenant. In meditation and before the Lord he thus repeats the experience of his people, but unlike them, he does not fail in his covenant obligations. Having succeeded where they failed, he is ready in his ministry as Messiah both to receive new revelation and to make known and available that revelation from God. In the wilderness Jesus is open to the guidance, help, and direction of the Holy Spirit in his digestion, of and obedience to, the Word of the Lord.

We thus may claim that the three temptations are three important and representative examples of victory by Jesus in his role and calling as the New Man, the new Israel, the Messiah. They are examples of victory over *basic* temptations to doubt, distrust, dishonor, and disobey the Lord. The point is that, though he was victorious through the power of the Spirit, the actual means of victory in each case was meditation on the inspired Word, the revealed will of God.

First, Jesus is fasting; he is hungry. He knows that, as the Messiah, he can call on the almighty power of God to assist him. Physically fit and a person who enjoys good food, he feels intensely the pangs of hunger. "Why not turn stones into food?" the Tempter says.

Jesus recalls the real physical hunger of the Israelites in the desert of Sinai and how God was seeking to teach them a lesson about dependence upon him and obedience to his revealed will (see Exod. 16; Num. 11). Already he has considered the Word of God which states, "Man does not live on bread alone but on every word that comes from the mouth of the LORD" (Deut. 8:3). He knows that perfect obedience to God and trust in him as Lord are the true means of sustenance of the people of God at all times in every situation—even when desperately hungry. In fact, such obedience and trust is more important than food— even food supernaturally produced (whether bread from stones or manna in the desert of Sinai). Jesus thus determines to live by the Word of God and to seek first the kingdom of God, knowing that all that is truly necessary will be given to him by the Father in heaven.

Second, Jesus is thinking about the role of Moses as God's prophet and leader of the Israelites from the exodus up to the entry into the land of Canaan. He recalls that Moses had prophesied that there would be another Prophet, greater than himself, who would truly declare the Word of the Lord (Deut. 18:14–22). Jesus knows that he is that Prophet. He pictures Moses on Mount Nebo being provided with a panoramic view of the promised land of Canaan (Deut. 34:1–4). Putting himself in Moses' sandals, Jesus too has a panoramic view—not merely of Palestine but of the whole world as the kingdom of God, filled with righteousness and mercy, with God's holy name being glorified by all everywhere, with truth and joy.

"To win that world for God," says Satan, "you will need to set your standards at a level that most people can reasonably reach. To do so isn't compromise; it's being sensible." This is the sinister temptation to discredit and subvert the command of God. Jesus recalls the constant temptation, faced by the Israelites in the desert and afterward, to adopt idolatry and thus be no better or worse than the people whom they encountered on their travels. He remembers how, soon after their being given the covenant at Sinai, the people became idolatrous. Thus he remembers and repeats to himself the basic command, "Fear the LORD your God, serve him only" (Deut. 6:13). He resolves and determines that as the Messiah he will be totally single-minded in the service of the Lord and will require the same of those whom he calls to be his disciples.

Third, Jesus is reflecting on his future ministry to his own people. How is he to make known the kingdom of God as a reality of the present and the future? Should he perform spectacular deeds such as jumping from the pinnacle of the temple in Jerusalem down into the gorge below in order to arrest their attention and reveal his supernatural powers? "A splendid idea," says Satan, "and God will take care of you, as Psalm 91 makes clear." But Jesus has already reflected on the attempts of Israel to put God to the test by demanding miraculous confirmation of his power (see Exod. 17:1–7; Num. 20:1–13). He has already meditated upon the command, "Do not test the LORD your God as you did at Massah" (Deut. 6:16). So he determines to trust and obey rather than to put the Lord to the test.

I do not mean to claim too much. The experience of Jesus in the wilderness was much more than a period of meditation: it was also lasting, spiritual struggle and victory, suffering, and communion with God in prayer. But meditation upon God's Word was near to the center of this profoundly spiritual experience which lasted over forty days and nights. Only in this way could Jesus, as Representative Man (new Adam and Messiah), take into his mind, heart, and will God's self-revelation and then be ready not only to overcome temptations but also to live in trust, obedience, and love of the Lord, his heavenly Father.

Furthermore, only by spiritually first digesting and then wholly appropriating that revelation which God had already given in various ways to his own people could Jesus begin to reveal more of God—his character, will, and grace—through his own personality and ministry. In other words, because he was to be the personal means through whom God enlarged the revelation he had already given through, and to, old Israel, he had to become the perfect recipient of, and responder to, that revelation. He had wholly to receive the old in order to bring in the new. In this process both of receiving afresh the revelation already given and of receiving and then giving to the world the new revelation establishing the new covenant, meditation was very important as the means whereby the Word of God moved from the mind to the heart and will.

At Caesarea Philippi

A prominent theme in the meditation of Jesus was undoubtedly the role, ministry, and destiny of the Messiah. He wanted to absorb everything that God had said on this theme to Israel through psalmist and prophet, king and sage, concerning the Anointed One. Since Jesus knew that it was his vocation to be the anointed King, Priest, and Prophet of the Lord, it was imperative that he fulfil this calling both in the way that God had promised and described as well as in loving obedience to, and communion with, his Father in heaven.

At the center of Mark's Gospel is the account of the visit that Jesus made at the halfway point in his ministry to the region of Caesarea Philippi. He took his disciples to this area on the slopes of Mount Hermon, a place with strong Roman associations, in order to share very important teaching with them. On arrival he asked them, "Who do people say I am?" They replied that some said he was John the Baptist returned from the dead and that others said he was a second Elijah. Yet others felt he was just a prophet. At this point he made his question very personal: "Who do you say I am?" (Mark 8:27–29).

The impulsive but insightful Peter had an instant answer. "You are the Messiah," he said, meaning that Jesus was the Man sent by God to be the leader of the people of Israel, to restore their fortunes in the world, to make

Jerusalem the center of worship for the whole world, and to realize salvation for the Jews.

Jesus of course had a good idea of what Peter and the others believed, and he knew that their view of the Messiah was much influenced by current Jewish teaching with its political overtones and longing of liberation from the Roman occupation. So he did not leave the matter there. He made a first attempt to share with his band of disciples the picture of the Messiah which he had in his own understanding and imagination and which was informing and guiding his own ministry. He made clear to them the results of his meditation and prayer.

The Messiah whom he describes is fully consistent with the verbal portrait which he heard at his baptism. "You are my Son, whom I love; with you I am well pleased" (Mark 1:11). In these words we may discern echoes of Psalm 2:7 (a Davidic, royal psalm) and Isaiah 42:1-2 (a prophecy concerning God's Servant). By the decree of the Father in heaven, Jesus is declared to be his Son (i.e., his Messiah) and to have a vocation which is described in Isaiah's prophecies concerning the Servant of the Lord (42:1-4; 49:1-6; 50:4-9; 52:13-53:12).

Using his chosen self-designation "Son of Man," Jesus explained that, because he was fulfilling the role of the Servant of the Lord, he had to suffer many things, be rejected by Judaism, be killed, and then rise from the dead. The last of the four Servant prophecies was of special importance in leading him to this insight and expectation. Instead of seeing the establishment of a cosmic, worldwide kingdom in this age and time, Jesus looked for vindication and the full reality of God's rule *after* he had suffered and been raised from death.

The idea that the Messiah had to suffer and die to fulfil his vocation was abhorrent to the disciples, schooled as they were in rather triumphalistic notions of the Messiah. So Peter, bold as ever, dared to rebuke Jesus for having said such a thing. This time, however, he had gone too far: he had become the mouthpiece for Satan by opposing what the prophets had foretold. Jesus spoke firmly to him.

The simple point I am making here is that the portrait of the Messiah which Jesus had adopted and which filled his understanding and imagination and guided his heart and will was arrived at, not through listening to popular religious talk, but by creative, penetrating, and prayerful meditation upon the Law and the Prophets of the Hebrew Bible. Much the same may be claimed for Jesus' teaching concerning his final vindication at his parousia, when he will come again in glory to judge both the living and the dead (Mark 8:38; 13:26; 14:62). It resulted from creative meditation on such passages as Daniel 7:8–28.

In the Garden of Gethsemane

As we noticed in our study of Psalm 77, it is possible—indeed necessary—to meditate in times of great stress and pressure. In such circumstances was the meditation/prayer of Jesus in the olive orchard known as Gethsemane on the eve of his crucifixion. The same circumstances ought to have led the disciples into meditation and prayer; regrettably, however, their physical need for sleep triumphed over their spiritual need to be spiritually alert.

The entry into the orchard of Jesus and the disciples Peter, James, and John is succinctly told in Mark 14:32–42. This passage repays careful study, meditation, and reflection. Jesus began to be deeply distressed and troubled, and he said to them: "My soul is overwhelmed with sorrow to the point of death. Stay here and keep watch." He was obviously appalled and profoundly troubled about what soon would be, and he expected his disciples to be aware of the crisis and to "watch" with him (i.e., spiritually awake).

Moving further into the orchard, Jesus fell to the ground and prayed to his Father that, if it were possible, the approaching hour might not come. "*Abba*, Father, everything is possible for you. Take this cup from me." Here we encounter a paradox of prayer. Jesus is entirely submitted to the Father (implied in his use of *Abba*, "dear Father"), but yet he asks that the "cup" be removed. This cup contains the judgment of God upon human rebellion and sin, and it is the cup which he, as Messiah and Suffering Servant, has to drink in order that the human race itself does not have to drink it. Jesus' meditation on the ministry and work of the Messiah has convinced him that he must suffer; but how can he take from his Father (with whom he has such intimate spiritual communion) the cup of divine wrath? He can and will only because this step is the Father's will.

As Jesus recalls the contents of the sacred Scriptures and their teaching about salvation through pain and suffering, death and hell, he gains the internal witness of spirit with the Holy Spirit that he is facing in the right direction and must place himself wholly in the Father's care as he continues to go forward. That his disciples do not seem to have any insight into what he is thinking, feeling, and anticipating is a further weight to the cross he now metaphorically bears and will soon literally have to carry.

Without going into detail, I believe that Jesus continued to pray and meditate even when he was on the cross. The seven sentences uttered by him on the cross reveal that he is recalling the content of the Hebrew Bible and using it to help him to pray and to die in perfect communion with the Father. The most obvious example is his great cry, "My God, my God, why have you forsaken me?" (Mark 15:34). This cry of dereliction is the cry of the One who is bearing and taking away the sin of the world. To know what was going on in the mind of Jesus, we need to read Psalm 22, from which it is a quotation. This passage, we may safely infer, was the basis for Jesus' thoughts as he suffered the indescribable anguish of drinking this cup of wrath (Jer. 49:12; cf. Isa. 51:17–23).

On Other Occasions

Though we confess that Jesus is the eternal Son of God made Man, the Word made flesh, we do not thereby minimize his human nature. To be truly human he must learn God's will for his life by the methods open to human beings—the study of Scripture, prayer, meditation, and contemplation in the context of living in trust, love, and obedience.

It may seem strange to us, but he who (as the eternal Son) is the final revelation of God to humankind also (as truly Man) had to receive that revelation for himself. And that reception, though marvelously guided and enabled by the Holy Spirit, was still according to the normal workings of the human personality, and began, of course, on Mary's knee and with Joseph's teaching at the table before meals and especially at the time of festivals. Mary herself was an adept meditator. We read that, on receiving the revelation from God that she was to be the mother of the Messiah, she "treasured up all these things and pondered them in her heart" (Luke 2:19). Joseph, too, knew also how to reflect on, consider, and obey the word of the Lord—as his marrying of the pregnant Mary reveals.

Apart from the very important example and influence of Mary and Joseph, Jesus was taught the Hebrew Bible at the local synagogue's school for boys. As was the custom, he both learned its contents by heart and received instruction in how to obey the law of God. We may thus conclude that, from his earliest years, he began to reflect on and spiritually to digest the Word of God. This practice is surely confirmed by the way in which he was able to discuss the Scriptures with the experts in Jerusalem when he was only twelve (Luke 2:41–50).

When we carefully read and reflect on the recorded teaching of Jesus in the four Gospels, we cannot avoid the conviction that Jesus was throughout his ministry constantly meditating on the Scriptures. He clearly loved,

knew, and had memorized the contents of the Hebrew
Bible, but his lively use of the sacred text and his profound
development of its teaching reveal much meditation. He
was not merely an excellent teacher; he brought forth
in his teaching revelation from God that had been spiritually and mentally digested through consideration and
reflection.

Consider, by way of example, two of the five blocks of
teaching provided in the Gospel of Matthew (chaps. 5–7,
10, 13, 18, 23–25). Reading through the familiar Sermon
on the Mount (chaps. 5–7), we recognize that such teaching has proceeded from a mind where it has been carefully
considered, examined, and studied and from a heart where
it has been appropriated as God's living truth. Themes
from the Hebrew Bible have been woven together and
given new emphasis; the light of the dawning kingdom of
God has shone into earlier insights in order to make them
into profound teaching.

Reading through the parables recorded in Matthew 13,
we find that Jesus must have been meditating upon God's
revelation in the created order as well as upon the response of the people to his own ministry. The parable of
the sower and the seed, and the explanation offered by
Jesus, could have been given only by a man who was
prayerfully reflective. The themes of the parables seem so
simple to us; however, their very simplicity and their purpose to evoke a moral response in the hearers reveal both
the teaching genius of Jesus and his constant meditation
and reflection.

The teaching in John's Gospel, such as Jesus' portrayal
of himself as the Shepherd, the Vine, the Way, the Truth,
the Life, the Resurrection, and the Light of the World indicates perhaps even more clearly Jesus' life of meditation. Also in John's Gospel we find an emphasis on the
profound communion between the Father and the Son,
the contemplation of the Father by the Son, and the great
desire of the Son to do the will of the Father. In the ex-

perience of Jesus, meditation is linked both to the Scriptures and to communion with the Father. It is never a dry-as-dust duty but is always a way into fellowship with heaven.

Jesus' Teaching on Meditation

Disciples were to learn from and imitate their Rabbi/ Master. The most important teaching Jesus gave to those who followed him was his personal example of meditation and prayer and of trust in and obedience to God, the Father. His actual words to them supplemented and buttressed his example of profound veneration for the revelation of God and constant meditation on it.

Regrettably, we may think, we learn virtually nothing about the personal devotions of the disciples from the four Gospels. Certainly they went to the synagogue each Sabbath and at festivals, and when in Jerusalem they attended the services in the temple. But what of their daily prayers? Did they pray together, with Jesus leading them? How did each one conduct his own devotions? We can only guess that they followed the Jewish practice of saying the appropriate daily prayers and that this exercise was expanded by what they learned from Jesus.

Certainly Jesus gave them teaching on prayer (e.g., Matt. 6:9–13; Luke 11:2–13; 18:10–14) and on loving, trusting, and communing with God as their heavenly Father. He enabled them to use the biblical prayer book, the Psalter, with new insight and commitment; and he enabled them to reflect on and consider the sacred Scriptures as a whole with a fresh vision and search for truth. Though we do not find any specific instruction on meditation, we find that, here and there in his teaching, Jesus commended, recommended, and commanded various aspects of meditation. In fact, he encouraged meditation in all kinds of ways, even though he did not present a method of meditation to disciples. Let us look at some of these teachings.

His Call to "Consider"

In the Sermon on the Mount there is not only the general encouragement to ponder the teaching of Jesus but also commands to consider specifically certain things. *"Look at* the birds of the air"; *"see* how the lilies of the field grow" (Matt. 6:26, 28; italics mine). Jesus also said, *"Watch out* for false prophets. . . . By their fruit you will recognize them" (Matt. 7:15–16, italics mine).

His Call to "Hear"

Jesus also encouraged meditation by inviting his audience to "hear." At the end of the Sermon on the Mount, Jesus refers to "everyone who hears these words of mine and puts them into practice" (Matt. 7:24). This "hearing" is obviously more than using the ears; it is also an internal digesting of the words so that they become the source and motivation of loving, informed action.

His Call to "See" and "Understand"

The purpose of the parables used by Jesus was to bring insight, illumination, and understanding, concerning the nature of the kingdom of God. By their very nature these forms of speech had the effect upon disciples of causing them to reflect, consider, think about, and meditate upon the truth being highlighted by the story, simile, or metaphor, with a view to obedience to God's will. Through the truth highlighted by parables, knowledge of "the secret of the kingdom of God" was given to them (Mark 4:11).

When explaining the meaning of the seed which fell on good ground to produce an abundant harvest, Jesus said that "others, like seed sown on good soil, hear the word, accept it, and produce a crop—thirty, sixty or even a hundred times what was sown" (Mark 4:20). Surely this illustration points to a reception by a mind that meditates on and a heart that submits to the Word. Mark 8:14–21 illuminates the mentality and understanding of the disciples, who had been a long time with Jesus as their Rabbi. Though they had witnessed God's power at work in his ministry (in particular, the marvelous feeding of the crowds), they still did not understand and appreciate the dynamic truth to which these miracles pointed. They had not digested in their minds and hearts what God was actually saying to them in the deeds and words of Jesus.

The Call to "Read"

On various occasions Jesus faced his critics, and before citing Scripture, he said to them, "Have you not read?" or similar words (see, e.g., Mark 11:17; 12:10, 26, 35–37). He was not merely calling for the actual reading of the text; he was also calling for meditation and reflection on the text.

His Call to "Remember"

We have already seen how important was the act of remembering within the faith and faithfulness of the Jews. When Jesus celebrated the Passover with his disciples (in which a key element is to remember the exodus from Egypt to Canaan) on the eve of his crucifixion, he also instituted the Lord's Supper. A key element in his instruction was "do this in *remembrance* of me" (Luke 22:19, italics mine). As Jews meditate on the exodus, so Christians are to meditate on the exodus of the crucifixion and resurrection of the Lord Jesus. Memory, understanding, and imagination are to be used in the service of receiving God's salvation in Jesus.

We may say that Jesus taught meditation not by a spoon-feeding method but by arousing the spiritual curiosity and aspirations of his disciples. He left it to others to provide methods by which genuine meditation could begin, continue, and flourish.

3

Under the New Covenant

Here we are concerned with Paul, apostle to the Gentiles under the new covenant, sealed with the blood of Jesus at Calvary. As a Pharisee, Saul of Tarsus knew thoroughly the text and contents of the Hebrew Bible. He was also familiar with Jewish writings outside the canon of that Bible (e.g., what we call the apocryphal Old Testament). Furthermore, he was an expert in the oral tradition of interpreting the law of Moses which was known as the tradition of the elders (see Mark 7:5–13; Phil. 3:4–6).

Since meditation on the torah is presented as basic to piety within the Psalter (Saul's prayer book), we may safely infer that Saul did meditate daily on the law, recalling its statutes, commandments, and ordinances from memory. It is possible also that he was familiar with and perhaps practiced the type of forced meditation known as *merkabah* (Heb. for "chariot"). In this method a person reflected on the chariot vision in Ezekiel 1 in order to be worked up to produce or receive similar apocalyptic visions. (See J. D. G. Dunn, "Let John be John," in *Das Evangelium, und die Evangeliene* [Tübergen: P. Stuhlmacher, 1983). (Some scholars think that Paul's visionary experience of being taken into the third heaven is of this kind [2 Cor. 12:2–4].)

Paul's Practice of Meditation

Saul the Pharisee was encountered by the exalted Lord Jesus Christ as Saul journeyed from Jerusalem to Damascus in order to persecute the young church there (Acts 9). This life-changing experience included the call to become the apostle to the non-Jewish peoples, the ambassador to the Gentile nations. Saul, the Jew, was to carry to them the Good News of God's salvation for all humankind, in, through, and with the Lord Jesus.

Saul, now Paul the apostle of Jesus, continued to meditate upon the contents of the Hebrew Bible as he had done in his career as a Pharisee. But he did so now with an enthusiasm, urgency, and power generated by the Holy Spirit, who both indwelt his soul and kept him in faith union with the Lord Jesus. As Jesus himself had gained from Scripture the direction for his ministry and passion, so Paul, his servant, began to gain from Scripture (the same Hebrew Bible) his portrait of Jesus as the Messiah and Lord, the only Mediator between God and humankind. In fact we may justly claim that a large part of Paul's epistles are the result of his meditation on the Bible as he sought to be a faithful apostle of Jesus in the Roman world.

Paul's Christology, for example, clearly indicates a life rich in meditation. Romans 5:12–21 (Jesus as the second and new Adam) suggests Paul's meditation upon Genesis 1–3, and 1 Corinthians 15:40–57 (the bodily resurrection of Jesus and his people) suggests meditation on Old Testament teaching about the new creation in Daniel 7:13 and Genesis 1:26. Paul's teaching in Romans 9–11, with its many citations from the Old Testament, truly reflects long and deep meditation on the place of the Jews in the purposes of God. This meditation may well have been given urgency and depth by his problems with the Judaizers, the results of whose teaching he faces in the Epistle to the Galatians.

Many Christians rightly think of Paul as the great teacher of the doctrine of justification by faith, certainly one of the central themes of his teaching. His doctrine of the righteousness of God, revealed in the gospel and given to those who believe in, and are united to, the Lord Jesus, is certainly inspired by his recalling of Abraham (the patriarch believed God, and his faith was counted to him for righteousness) and of the teaching in Isaiah about the righteousness and salvation of God to be revealed in the last days (especially in chaps. 40–66). We may say that, as Paul prayerfully meditated on the Hebrew Bible (or its Greek translation, the Septuagint), the exalted Lord Jesus from heaven, through the Holy Spirit, shared that meaning of the sacred text with Paul that was in his own mind. Then, as far as righteousness is concerned, Paul had to express that meaning in the Epistles to the Galatians and the Romans.

We do not know at what times of day and night Paul meditated. It is obvious, however, that he would have opportunities on his travels to make the space and time in early morning and in the evening for meditation and prayer. Furthermore, as journeys were slow, the actual journeying would also provide opportunity for reflection, consideration, and meditation. We can easily picture Paul's using the time profitably, whether to witness for Jesus or to meditate and pray.

Paul's primary aim, of course, was not to meditate but to be an effective apostle to the Gentiles and to live in constant communion with the Lord Jesus through the Spirit. He wanted to know God in Jesus not merely at the level of theological understanding but in the experience of personal fellowship and mystical union. "I want to know Christ and the power of his resurrection and the fellowship of sharing in his sufferings, becoming like him in his death, and so, somehow, to attain to the resurrection from the dead" (Phil. 3:10–11). In comparison with knowing

Christ Jesus the Lord, every other experience and form of knowledge was like rubbish!

The apostle did not want his converts merely to meditate; he wanted them to know, love, and serve God through Jesus Christ in the power of the Spirit. He constantly prayed for them.

> I keep asking that the God of our Lord Jesus Christ, the glorious Father, may give you the Spirit of wisdom and revelation, so that you may know him better. I pray also that the eyes of your heart may be enlightened in order that you may know the hope to which he has called you, the riches of his glorious inheritance in the saints, and his incomparably great power for us who believe. [Eph. 1:17–19]

In order to have the eyes of the heart enlightened and to know the dynamic nature of the Christian hope, meditation involving memory, understanding, and imagination was required. So we move on to Paul's teaching on the subject.

Paul's Teaching on Meditation

In order to appreciate what the apostle has to say about meditation, we shall look at his use of five words in particular context. Then I shall attempt to summarize what we have seen.

His Call to "Think"

The verb *phroneō* means "to form or hold an opinion, set one's mind on, be disposed toward." It signifies a combination of intellectual and affective activity of both understanding and heart, leading to a course of action. It expresses not merely an activity of the intellect but also a movement of the will; it is thus both interest and decision at the same time. A modern example of how this verb functions is the following: I *consider* the programs of the political parties; I *desire* one of them above the others; I *go out* both to vote for that party and to encourage others to do so as well. Thus *phroneō* covers the consideration, the desire, and the action.

It is not surprising that Paul often uses this verb to urge the members of the churches to "live in harmony with one another" or to "be of one mind" (e.g., Rom. 12:16; 15:5; 2 Cor. 13:11; Phil. 2:2; 4:2; Gal. 5:10). In these verses, the verb refers to a common Christian attitude and action, proceeding from a shared understanding of, and meditation upon, the gospel.

The process of digesting the living word of God in mind and heart in order to guide the will is presupposed by Paul's use of *phroneō* in Romans 8:5–6.

> Those who live according to the sinful nature *have their minds set* on what that nature desires; but those who live in accordance with the Spirit *have their minds set* on what the Spirit desires. The *mind* of the sinful man is death, but the *mind* controlled by the Spirit is life and peace. [italics mine]

Here we note that Paul assumes that human nature is sinful and that, without the presence and direction of the indwelling Spirit, it will act contrary to God's will. People who have not been born from above and in whom the Spirit of Christ does not dwell thus cannot either think or do what is pleasing to God. However sophisticated their thoughts and speech, mind, and action, they remain natural beings who are not supernaturally united to the Lord Jesus Christ through the Spirit. In contrast, a baptized believer, in whom dwells the Spirit of Christ, is enabled through the help of that Spirit both to pay attention to and to seek to do the will of God. The Spirit comes from the exalted Lord Jesus, bearing his name and bringing his virtue; the believer has thus special help to receive, digest, and to do what is pleasing to God. Because of the Spirit's help, the believer's mind and heart are raised to a higher level of activity; they are now enabled to consider, reflect on, and appropriate the living truth of the gospel.

Later in the Epistle to the Romans, Paul makes it clear that meditation inspired by the Spirit is characterized by the virtue of humility. In 11:20, within the discussion of the place of Gentile believers in the purposes of God, he urges them, "Do not be arrogant, but be afraid" (i.e., have reverence for God). A little later he urges, "Do not think of yourself more highly than you ought, but rather think of yourself with sober judgment, in accordance with the measure of faith God has given you" (Rom. 12:3). Note that this last reference to humility follows the call to be "transformed by the renewing of your mind" (v. 2).

How can such humility be attained? Certainly it is the result of the gracious work of the Spirit in the mind and heart, and certainly also it results from prayerful meditation on the example of Christ himself. In Philippians 2:5, Paul introduces his poem/hymn on the humility of Christ with the words "have this mind," or "your attitude should be" (literally "think ye this"). Paul uses *phroneō* again in 3:15 to encourage correctness in thinking, meditation, and attitude. He writes literally, "Let us think this," in reference to the call of the gospel to press on to the perfection of love, trust, and obedience.

Finally, consider the use of *phroneō* in Colossians 3:2, where Paul calls for meditation upon Christ in the heavenly realm, for there he is enthroned as Lord. "Since, then, you have been raised with Christ, set your hearts on things above, where Christ is seated at the right hand of God. *Set your minds* on things above, not on earthly things. For you died, and your life is now hidden with Christ in God" (italics mine). The phrase "set your hearts" in verse 1 is the verb *zēteō*, which means "to seek (from the heart)." Here it is pointing to the heavenly orientation of the human will and desires.

By causing their thoughts to dwell on the reality of the exalted Lord, Paul believes that their desires will be strengthened to serve Jesus as Lord in this world. And, we may agree, it is most appropriate that Christians cause their minds and hearts to focus on the exalted Lord in his heavenly glory, since their life "is now hidden with Christ in God." Being in the body of Christ, in intimate spiritual union with him, they in a sense are already in heaven. Meanwhile on earth in their old, physical bodies, they are sojourners and pilgrims moving toward their final, heavenly existence in the kingdom of God of the age to come.

His Call to "Count"

Logizomai, "to reckon, calculate, evaluate, consider, ponder, let one's mind dwell on," is used some thirty-four times by Paul. It is his particular favorite to convey what God does for the believing sinner because of the righteousness of Jesus Christ, the Mediator. God *counts* his or her faith for righteousness, *reckoning* to that individual the righteousness of Christ, in whom he or she lives by the Spirit. What God counts and reckons he also fulfils and will fulfil, for decision, word, and act belong together with God.

On a few occasions, the Christian is the subject of the verb, and here again we are to understand that decision, word, and act belong together, so that the reckoning, or counting, is an act of mind, heart, and will. Such is obviously the case in Romans 6:11–12, where Paul, on the basis of his explanation of the believer's union with Christ in his death and resurrection, writes in this way: "*Count* yourselves dead to sin but alive to God in Christ Jesus. Therefore do not let sin reign in your mortal body" (italics mine). Christians meditate on their spiritual union with Christ and, in the power of the Holy Spirit, go forth to live as those who are actually mortifying sin and living in, and for, righteousness.

Later in Romans the apostle provides us with an insight

into his own meditation. He looked forward to the new created order of the kingdom of God to follow the second coming of Christ, and in the light of this hope he could gladly suffer now for Christ's sake. "I *consider* that our present sufferings are not worth comparing with the glory that will be revealed in us. The creation waits in eager expectation for the sons of God to be revealed" (8:18–19, italics mine). Paul's commitment and energy were refreshed by regular contemplation of God's glorious future plans for the cosmos and redeemed humanity.

In several places in 1 Corinthians and Philippians, Paul uses the verb *logizomai* in a way that includes or presupposes meditation. He teaches that, in their thoughts and prayers, church members ought to know how to think about him and his colleagues who are devoted to the ministry of the gospel. "Men ought *to regard* us as . . . those entrusted with the secret things of God" (1 Cor. 4:1, italics mine). Furthermore, in thinking about other people, a loving Christian *"keeps no record* of wrongs"* (1 Cor. 13:5, italics mine). If meditation proceeds on sound principles, then one's prayer and attitude will also be sound.

In the progressive path of holiness in the pilgrimage toward God in Christ, meditation which includes a right evaluation of oneself together with an adventurous, bold looking to Christ is indispensable. Paul's own testimony was as follows:

> I press on to take hold of that for which Christ Jesus took hold of me. Brothers, I do not *consider* myself yet to have taken hold of it. But one thing I do: Forgetting what is behind and straining toward what is ahead, I press on toward the goal to win the prize for which God has called me heavenward in Christ Jesus [Phil. 3:12–14, italics mine]

Here is holy enthusiasm fired by meditation!

Furthermore, we have a duty to discipline our minds to consider and dwell upon that which is pleasing to God.

"Finally, brothers, whatever is true, whatever is noble, ... whatever is admirable—if anything is excellent or praiseworthy—*think about* such things" (Phil. 4:8, italics mine). We may call this requirement a basic rule for meditation.

His Call to "See"

The verb *skopeō* means "to fix one's gaze on, concentrate one's attention on." Paul uses this verb only on a few occasions, but there is one telling and important use of it in 2 Corinthians 4:16–18. There he writes:

> Though outwardly we are wasting away, yet inwardly we are being renewed day by day. For our light and momentary troubles are achieving for us an eternal glory that far outweighs them all. So *we fix our eyes* not on what is seen, but on what is unseen. [italics mine]

Paul has in mind the unseen Lord Jesus Christ seated at the Father's right hand in glory and present in his body on earth in and through the Holy Spirit, the Spirit of Christ. *Skopeō* is stronger than *blepō* ("to look") and points to the consideration and reflection which becomes contemplation, where the heart is fixed in loving adoration on God, as Christ (through the imagination) is seen in all his glorious excellence by the eyes of faith.

His Call to "Gird"

Basically, *perizōnnymi* means "to gird or bind around." Paul was totally convinced that the Christian community was in a situation of war against Satan, evil, and sin. As soldiers of Christ, believers are to have their proper equipment and clothing: they are to be armed in order to fight and to win. Using the Roman soldier's dress and armor for illustrative purposes, Paul described the spiritual clothing and armor of the Christian in his or her role as a soldier (Eph. 6:10–18). Urging Christians to put on the full armor of God, he reminded them that the first job was to have the belt of truth *buckled around* the waist. The belt was a long piece of leather, suitably reinforced, used for tucking up the outer dress in order to facilitate walking and fighting. It enabled one to move and act like a soldier.

The Christian soldier is to wear the belt of truth. The teaching of the gospel must continually inform the mind, uplift the heart, and motivate the will. To gird oneself around with such a belt involves hearing, receiving, reading, digesting, appropriating, and obeying God's truth as it is presented in the gospel of God concerning Jesus Christ.

We have looked at four verbs. Others which would yield much the same kind of insights are *ginōskō* ("to know"; see 1 Cor. 13:12; Gal. 4:9), *epekteinomai* ("to stretch forward"; see Phil. 3:13), *mimnēskomai* ("to recall to mind"; see 1 Cor. 11:2; 2 Tim. 1:4), and *mnēmoneuō* ("to remember"; see Gal. 2:10; Eph. 2:11). The fifth key word in Paul's teaching on meditation is the noun *elpis*, "hope."

His Call to "Hope"

Within the New Testament the main emphasis upon hope is in the epistles of Paul. The apostle fills out the testimony of the Hebrew Bible, which often commands us to "hope in the LORD" or to "wait for the LORD." Hope, whatever its fullest definition, certainly includes a cognitive activity which effects a permanent change in our life here on earth. Hope is strengthened and increased through meditation on the Lord as he is revealed to us in the Bible. Paul knew the importance of having genuine hope in mind and heart, and he prayed: "May the God of *hope* fill you with all joy and peace as you trust in him, so that you may overflow with *hope* by the power of the Holy Spirit" (Rom. 15:13, italics mine; cf. 2 Thess. 2:16). However, since Jesus Christ is our *hope* (1 Tim. 1:1; cf. Col. 1:27), the heart overflows with hope only as it is centered upon, meditating on, and trusting in the Lord Jesus.

What we look for and await in the future is defined with reference to the One who has already come to reveal God to us.

Hope is a patient, disciplined, and humbly confident waiting for, and eager expectation of, the parousia (appearance in glory) of the Lord Jesus to bring an end to this evil age and inaugurate the new one. It is a movement of the mind and heart toward God's goal of full salvation (1 Thess. 5:8), perfect righteousness (Gal. 5:5), eternal life (Titus 1:2; 3:7), and an immortal resurrection body in the glory of God (Rom. 5:2; Col. 1:27; 2 Cor. 3:12). Those who have this hope are very willing to make sacrifices in order to gain its fulfilment (see Rom. 5:2–5; 8:22–25; 2 Cor. 5:6–10; Phil. 1:18–26).

Without some kind of hope, people in ordinary living would collapse and not be able to accept the work of day to day. Even if the hope is merely for an event such as a birthday or Christmas or a family reunion, it has the power to generate energy to press on. The more these hoped-for events are thought about, the more they give energy and desire. In a much more profound way, the same is true of Christian hope. The more it is thought about, or the more the God who is its center is thought about, the more is hope produced in the heart. Hope encourages meditation, and also meditation increases hope, especially since the Christian hope has definite content and is fully open to the use of the understanding and imagination (as the holy dreams of John in Rev. 21–22 testify).

Paul's writings contain no simple, distinct concept of meditation. Rather, meditation is contained in a larger amalgamation of concepts, linked together as the parts of a chain or the colors of the rainbow. In other words, Paul is wholly committed to the practice of meditation but not as a single, isolated duty. It is a duty before God which is inextricably united to the hearing, receiving, remembering, and recalling of the truth; to the work of the Spirit in the heart and mind; to the obeying of the gospel; to trust in God; and to loving and serving him in Christ's name.

Paul puts great emphasis on the necessity of the renewal of the mind because from the mind the heart and will are guided and inspired. In Ephesians 4, Paul is very insistent on the renewal of the mind. Before the Gentiles were enlightened by the gospel and illuminated within by the Holy Spirit, they were darkened in their understanding and ignorant of divine reality with hardened hearts. They were to be "made new in the attitude of their minds" (v. 23); an important part in this process was meditation.

In meditation we are to assume that Paul used and expected others to use the full powers of memory, understanding, and imagination. It takes imagination to meditate on the heavenly realm, where Christ is in glory, or upon the new heaven and earth of the kingdom of God, which shall be after the parousia of Christ. It also takes imagination to consider, for example, "the riches of his glorious inheritance in the saints, and his incomparably great power for us who believe" (Eph. 1:18–19). And the way in which Paul discusses doctrine shows that he was altogether in favor of using the intellect and understanding. Let us never forget, however, that Paul's heart and will were never separated from his mind, and he wanted to know experientially and in obedience the truth of the teaching he had received and which he also gave.

4

Biblical Teaching

It will be helpful at this stage to pull together the various strands of teaching on meditation from the Old and New Testaments. Such a summary can clarify our thinking about biblical meditation and can allow us to see better how it differs from Eastern methods of meditation, which are becoming increasingly widespread and are often commended under a Christian banner. There is the further important reason that, if we know what biblical meditation is, then we know what God is calling us to practice.

Meditation and the Mind

Meditation is particularly an activity of the mind—the memory, understanding, and imagination. It involves both recalling/remembering and considering/pondering God's Word and deeds with a view to making an appropriate response of heart and will. It is an examining of the text of Scripture as a disciple, servant, and witness of Jesus Christ. It involves the intellect, which does not mean that it is only for so-called intellectuals. Ordinary people who use their minds for everyday purposes in doing their work and solving their problems are to use the same mind (led and illuminated by the Spirit of Christ) in their meditation. In meditation the mind is subservient to God in creaturely humility and is expecting to be instructed and inspired by him.

Meditation and God

Meditation is always on God in his self-revelation. Since God is the Creator, he is revealed in the natural order; since God is the Lord and Judge, he is revealed in history. Apart from this general revelation of his eternal deity, God has revealed his character, will, and purposes in his relationship to Israel, in and through Jesus Christ, and by the apostles of Jesus. The record of this special revelation is the sacred Scriptures.

To meditate is to consider, ponder, and reflect on one or another aspect of this divine self-disclosure. Thus it can begin from a viewing of the natural world, a consideration of historical events, a portion of the sacred text, a theme of the Bible, or a summary of a theme in a creed or confession of faith. In other words, meditation always has a content—it is the fixing of the powers of the mind on God as he is revealed to us. Its natural consequence is therefore prayer and active obedience.

The Frequency of Meditation

Meditation is a daily exercise, in two ways. Throughout each day, wherever we may be, there are many opportunities to ponder and reflect (howbeit briefly) upon one or another aspect of God's revelation in his creation and providence or to focus one's memory upon a scriptural theme. In the second place, there is the fixed time for meditation in the morning and/or evening, when a definite, disciplined attempt is made to consider God's special revelation in Word and deed in order to draw near to him as Father and Lord, Savior and Master.

It is as appropriate to meditate and pray each day as it is to eat and drink, to sleep and to work. The difference is that (for most of us) it is easier to eat, drink, work, and sleep than it is to meditate and pray. But these spiritual exercises become a joy as we grow into the practice of them.

There is no definite teaching as to the place of meditation. In an agricultural economy a favorite spot was out in the fields, but others made use of their homes (climbing perhaps onto the roof), the temple, and synagogues.

Meditation and Silence

Meditation will normally proceed in silence and may include or lead to silence of the heart. One advantage of going out into the fields for the Israelite was that it was quiet. In the Sermon on the Mount Jesus spoke of the need to find a quiet place (Matt. 6:5–8). From the contents of the Psalter we can deduce that the psalmists meditated in a variety of places, including the courts of the temple in Jerusalem, where they could be alone with God.

Apart from the quiet surroundings, there is also the gaining of a quiet mind and heart, an inner stillness of spirit. In the considerations of God's Word, the meditator may be overcome by awe and wonder or by abasement and humility. There is the stillness of reverence and the stillness of repentance; there is also the quietness of simply waiting for and upon the Lord. Such considerations underline the fact that meditation cannot easily be separated from prayer and adoration.

Meditation and Prayer

Meditation cannot be separated from prayer. This statement is true both of general meditation throughout the day as well as for fixed meditation at specific times. We are called both to meditate day and night and to pray without ceasing. We believe that God is omnipresent and that in him we live and move and have our being.

A brief meditation in the day may therefore well lead to an "arrow" prayer, just as in fixed meditation short prayers will begin, accompany, and interpenetrate the exercise. Following fixed meditation, the heart will be moved to one or more of the different aspects of prayer (depending on the nature of the meditation)—praise, thanksgiving, confession, petition, and intercession. In some cases the soul will be so caught up in fellowship with God that the person will feel wholly taken over with a sense of wonder, love, and praise.

Meditation and All Believers

Meditation is a duty for all, whatever point they have reached in the way of holiness toward perfection. Unless a person is sick, mentally retarded, or otherwise incapacitated, he or she has a duty to meditate. We recall that Jesus was found meditating in the Garden of Gethsemane on the eve of his crucifixion. We recall that Paul the apostle, who was earnestly pressing forward toward the high mark of perfection in union with Christ Jesus, felt the necessity of meditation to help him on that holy journey.

Of course, we can pray to God without first meditating on God's revelation, and there will be many occasions when we need to pray and cannot wait to meditate. However, in order to ensure that our relationship with God is experientially two-sided (God's speaking to us as well as our speaking to him), meditation is necessary. In this exercise the exalted Lord Jesus speaks to us through the Spirit, making use of the written Word of God, which is Scripture.

Meditation and the Christian Life

Meditation prepares the believer for the daily fight against the world, the flesh, and the devil and for the service of God in the loving of the neighbor. As food and drink nourish the body so that it can fight disease and be at the direction of the human will to do what is right, so the reception into the soul of the Word of God nourishes it and prepares a person to be and do what is pleasing to God.

Meditation and Worship

Meditation is particularly appropriate in the context of corporate worship in the sacred and holy place. Not a few of the psalms were composed in the temple, where the writers were meditating. Isaiah received his call to be a prophet as he meditated in the temple (Isa. 6). Jews were expected to meditate on the contents of the Law and Prophets when they were read in the synagogue. And Jesus called the temple a house of prayer (i.e., meditation and prayer). Furthermore, there is the marvelous portrayal in the imaginative language of symbolism and apocalyptic of heavenly worship in the meditation of John, writer of the last book of the Bible.

Meditation and Groups

Finally, meditation can occur in the company of others under the direction of a teacher. In the Old Testament we have the description of the prophet and his followers and the wise man and his students. In the New Testament there is the presentation of Jesus, the traveling Rabbi, surrounded by his disciples and also of the apostles accompanied by assistants and helpers. In all these cases, as teaching was given, those who heard were being invited to reflect upon, to consider, to imagine, and to act on the knowledge of God's will being disclosed to them.

There is very little teaching in the Bible about the technique of meditation and prayer. It is assumed that, to meditate and pray effectually, a person needs a reasonably quiet place and needs to be without major discomfort. But nothing is said about the control of breathing or the right posture, for such matters were seen as very much secondary to the experiencing of the living God.

In the Eastern methods and techniques (as taught in the West), much emphasis is placed on posture, breathing, poised awareness, and right place without distractions. And then the meditation is usually in one of the following forms:

1. Fixing the attention on the breathing, which should be abdominal; counting each exhalation up to ten and then continuing this procedure for twenty minutes.
2. Concentrating on following the flow of the breathing but without counting; being aware of the swelling and drawing in of the abdomen and doing so for twenty minutes.
3. Gazing in a fixed way at any object that is a pleasant or neutrally visual stimulus and from time to time closing the eyes to gaze upon the image of that object; continuing for twenty minutes.
4. Being quietly aware of any sound that is either a pleasant or neutrally auditory stimulus and remaining aware for twenty minutes.
5. Silently repeating a word (mantra) for twenty minutes.

The differences between the biblical approach and Eastern methods are obvious, as was stated in the Preface. Meditation in a Christian sense is meditating on the objective, revealed Word of God and includes the *full use of the capacities of the mind.* Such meditation may well lead to the silence of reverence and awe but never to a vague kind of mystical consciousness.

2

Examples of Method

5

The Evangelical Way

After the invention of printing, both Roman Catholic and Protestant authors produced, throughout the sixteenth and seventeenth centuries, a steady flow of books on the topic, "How to meditate and pray," often containing examples of meditations. Catholic authors include Ignatius of Loyola, founder of the Jesuits (*Spiritual Exercises*, 1523), and Francis de Sales, exiled bishop of Geneva (*Introduction to a Devout Life*, 1608); Protestant writers include Joseph Hall, bishop of Norwich (*The Art of Divine Meditation*, 1606, and *Meditation and Vows*, 1605–1606), and Richard Baxter, a Puritan pastor (*The Saints' Everlasting Rest*, 1650). Such authors made use of the traditions of meditation and prayer established in the religious communities and written in books by theologians and spiritual directors.

Certain basic characteristics are found in this literature, whether Catholic or Protestant. First, meditation is seen as an activity of the human understanding or imagination with reference to Christian truth (found in the Bible or a creed). Second, such meditation is seen as being a preparation for prayer because it creates a desire for God in a heart that is being prepared to worship, trust, and obey him. Truth considered in the mind in the presence of God warms the heart and so paves the way for communion with God. And third, meditation (like prayer) is presented as a daily duty.

In general, we may assume that those who produced books on meditation did so with the purpose of leading us from thinking about God and his will to loving him and praying to him as our God in order to be his true disciple and faithfully serve him. In meditation we move from thinking, reasoning, reflecting, and remembering to looking unto and longing for God in his glory and holiness, power, and love so that we may be his loving, obedient people.

In order to appreciate the methods of meditation found in this literature, we need to remember that both Catholic and Protestant writers faced the same situation in Europe—universal nominal Christianity. Apart from a few Jews and Muslims, everyone was a baptized person. Within this general commitment to Christianity, there was a sizable minority who took their faith seriously and wanted to be wholehearted, committed Christians. Such individuals, moved by the preaching of either the Protestant Reformation or the Catholic (Counter) Reformation, began to discover what conversion to God-in-Christ really meant through the daily discipline of meditation and prayer. Whereas converts to Christ in the apostolic period came into the churches with a desire (created by their experience of regeneration and conversion) to pray and meditate and needed guidance how to do so, baptized people in Europe in the sixteenth century often discovered the God of grace and converting power through meditation and prayer. Those who wrote on basic meditation had this experience in mind and so aimed to bring people not only to conversion but also to convertedness. In fact, all books on meditation must be for "beginners" (using the word in its widest sense), since those who become proficient in the discipline of meditation do not need any longer to refer to books for help with method. Someone who has developed the art of meditation may indeed benefit from looking at a book containing descriptions of methods he or she does not personally use. Generally, however, help with method is by its nature aimed at beginners or those who want to make a fresh start.

When meditation is described as discursive mental prayer, it sounds dry as dust and totally cerebral. Such is not the case, however. Meditation is described as discursive (especially by Roman Catholic writers) in order to make a distinction between meditation and contemplation. The latter is presented as being simple in the sense that it is the loving attention of the whole soul upon God in a simple way; that is, the mind is not engaged in considering this or that truth about God or imagining this or that part of the life of Christ. The whole inner self is quiet and still and looking only unto God in a state of utter reverence, total admiration, and wholehearted worship and adoration. Meditation, or mental prayer, is thus the activity of the mind, heart, and will before the Lord, seeking to draw near to him and do his will, while contemplation is a higher stage of being raised (by the Holy Spirit) into a simple, loving attention to God.

Not all writers on meditation accept this distinction. Many Protestants used the terms *meditation* and *contemplation* as virtually synonymous, while agreeing that the activity of reflecting, considering, and pondering ought to lead on to prayer that should include deep union and communion with God himself through Christ and by the Spirit. Through the influence of such writers as St. John of the Cross (1542–1591) and St. Teresa of Avila (1515–1582) and the anonymous English book *The Cloud of Unknowing* (written in the fourteenth century), contemplation and contemplative (or mystical) prayer have been seen, especially by some Catholics, as a type of prayer much superior to prayer that uses the discursive intellect. In contrast, Protestants have always insisted that, since the Scriptures are God's written Word to us, the surest way to approach him and to contemplate his attributes

and glory is to begin with meditation on the sacred Scriptures, the pages open before one's eyes. Short cuts to the
simple gazing on God and to a state of being lost in wonder, love, and praise are therefore not encouraged. The
holiest seekers after God ought to begin with God's holy
Word and let the Spirit of the exalted Lord Jesus lead
them on in communion with their Lord.

In the rest of this chapter we shall examine a simple
method of meditation and prayer suggested by Martin
Luther in the early period of the Protestant Reformation
in Germany. Then in chapter 6 we shall look at a method
devised for Catholic laity by St. Peter of Alcántara
(1499–1562). He was a leader of the Counter Reformation
in Spain and was, by all accounts, a wise and holy man.
Peter's method is more demanding than that of the Lutheran tradition. However, Protestants soon also came up
with more demanding and complex methods than Luther
had recommended. I discuss one such method in chapter 7—the Puritan way, developed in England and New
England in the first half of the seventeenth century.

After surveying three different methods of individual
meditation, we shall turn in chapter 8 to notice two methods of group meditation used in the twentieth century in
Europe and North America. These operate on the same
principle as a group prayer meeting or Bible study: what
you do alone you can do together, and what you do together you can do alone. Finally, in an Epilogue, I shall
set out a basic method of meditation for those who want
to start with something (which they can revise or modify)
and also offer some general comments on how to begin
and continue the discipline of meditation as a way of
drawing closer to God and experiencing his drawing closer
to us.

Luther's Way of Meditation

The aim of the Protestant minister (whether in Geneva,
Augsburg, or London) was to persuade his parishioners to

repent of their sins, to embrace the gospel by saving faith, and to live faithful, trusting, and obedient lives for God's glory. Thereby they would fulfil the covenant promises made for them by their sponsors at their (infant) baptism. For, as Luther often insisted, the Christian life is living out the implications of the reality, "I have been baptized."

This Christian life of faith and faithfulness had to be lived in the world where there was evil and Satan, sin and sorrow. To be daily fortified and prepared to fight as Christ's soldiers and love as his brothers, Christian believers had to feed on the Word of God to nourish their souls and to pray to the Lord for strength and guidance. On the Lord's Day they had to gather with their fellow Christians for the ministry of the Word and sacrament in the public church. Daily meditation on the sacred text and in the presence of the Lord was thus a basic duty and discipline done out of need, gratitude, and love.

In 1535 Martin Luther was asked by his barber, Peter Beskendorf, for some practical help on how to compose himself for prayer. Luther gladly agreed to share his thoughts and produced a booklet which he called, *A Simple Way to Pray, for a Good Friend* (1535). It could have been entitled "a simple way to meditate," for it is about meditation and prayer. In fact, the booklet contains Luther's own method—reading, reflection, considering what the Holy Spirit is saying to him, and then prayer.

Luther's method was widely used within Lutheranism and was given careful articulation by many pastors. In his *Paved Way to Peace in God*, Caspar Calvöt (1650–1725) described the Lutheran method as "the ladder of devotion" or "the heavenly ladder." This ladder is the fruitful use of divine truth through daily meditation, self-examination, and prayer, guided and assisted by the Spirit of Christ. I describe it below in the first person.

1. *Preparation.* I set apart at least fifteen minutes every day in a quiet place, preferably in the morning.

2. *Reading of Scripture.* I read the appointed lesson(s)

for the day. Today it is John 3. Before I read I ask God to illuminate my mind and heart and to bend my will to his will.

3. *Choice of short portion.* Having carefully read the whole lesson, I choose a significant paragraph or verse from the whole. My choice is the much-quoted verse 16: "For God so loved the world that he gave his one and only Son, that whoever believes in him shall not perish but have eternal life." I read this verse three or four times slowly, deliberately, and reverently, believing that in and through it the Lord Jesus will speak to me by his Spirit.

4. *Questions to ask of the text.* To help uncover its meaning for me, I ask a series of basic questions (who, what, where, and why). Looking at John 3:16, I ask:

Who has loved the world?

What does it mean that he gave his one and only Son?

Where did this divine giving take place?

Why do people of this world need eternal life?

Why am I to believe in God's one and only Son?

I answer these questions, conscious that I am in the presence of the Lord Jesus.

5. *Recollection.* In the process of answering these questions, I recall from memory all that I have been taught in creed and catechism, sermon and liturgy, hymn and prayer, Old and New Testaments, which provides information to answer these questions. I do not allow my mind to wander all over the globe of possibilities: I seek to concentrate on the questions.

6. *Consideration.* I carefully consider what teaching I am receiving from God as I take the meaning of John 3:16 into my heart and mind. Whether it is a word of encouragement or chastisement, comfort or command, I seek to consider it carefully and reverently.

7. *Self-examination.* Because the written Word of God is a word to me through the operation of the Spirit of the Lord Jesus, my consideration of the text includes self-examination. Do I really appreciate how much God loves the human race? Am I truly aware of the cost to God himself of sending his one and only Son to live and die for me? Am I truly and firmly believing the good news concerning Jesus, the one and only Son? Have I received the gift of eternal life? Do I seek to make the gospel known to others? And so forth.

8. *Prayer and communion with God.* Since my heart is now warmed and inspired by the love of God and since my mind is illuminated by the truth of the gospel, I can begin to pray—to love and adore God, to thank and praise him, to confess my sins to him, and to offer petitions and intercession to him in the name of Jesus.

This method is attractive in its simplicity and will be most effective when used every day by serious-minded people who are committed members of a Christian congregation. Those who use Bible-reading notes will have to make certain adjustments to use this method with such notes, but there is no reason why the two methods should not be combined. Those who meditate in this "Lutheran way" will either become less dependent on the devotional thoughts of authors of notes or will use them creatively to deepen their own recollection, consideration, and self-examination. One real problem with using notes is that they can lead to a spoon-feeding mentality. (See "Additional Note" below.)

Müller's Recommendation of Meditation

I add here a testimony to the value of basic, evangelical meditation from the pen of George Müller (1805–1898). His early training in Christian theology was in Lutheranism before he became a leader within the movement called "the Open Brethren." He is chiefly remembered for the orphanage he founded in Bristol, England. He described his practice of meditation in *Soul Food* (London, 1897). Whether he was aware of the earlier Lutheran teaching on meditation is not clear; what he adopted is very much like it.

> It has pleased the Lord to teach me a truth, the benefit of which I have not lost for fourteen years. I saw more clearly than ever that the first business to which I ought to attend every day, was to have my soul happy in the Lord. The first thing to be concerned about, was not how much I might serve the Lord, but how I might get my soul in a happy state, and how my inner man might be nourished. I might seek truth to set it before the unconverted. I might seek to benefit believers, I might seek to relieve the distressed, and I might in other ways seek to behave myself as it becomes a child of God in this world, and yet, not being happy in the Lord, and not being strengthened in the inner man day by day, all this might not be attended to in the right spirit.
>
> Before this time my practice had been to give myself to prayer after having dressed in the morning. Now I saw the most important thing I had to do was to give myself to the reading of the Word of God, and to *meditate* on it, thus my heart might be comforted, encouraged, warned, reproved, instructed, and that thus, by means of the Word of God, my heart might be brought into experimental communion with the Lord.
>
> I began therefore to *meditate* on the New Testament from the beginning, early in the morning. The first thing I did after having asked in a few words the Lord's blessing upon his Word, was to begin to meditate on the Word, searching, as it were, every verse to get a blessing out of it . . . not for the sake of public ministry, not preaching, but for obtaining food for my soul.
>
> The result I found to be invariably this. After a few minutes my soul had been led to confession, or thanksgiving, or intercession, or supplication, yet it turned almost immediately to prayer. When thus I have been for a while making confession, or intercession, or supplica-

tion or having given thanks, I go to the next words of the verse, turning all as I go into prayer for myself or others, as the Word may lead to it, but still continually keeping before me that food for my own soul as the object of my meditation.

The difference, then, between my present practice and my former is this. Formerly, when I arose, I began to pray as soon as possible, and generally spent all my time till breakfast in prayer, or almost all the time. At all events I almost invariably began with prayer, except when I felt my soul to be more than usually barren, in which case I would read the Word. But what was the result? I often spent a quarter of an hour, or half an hour, or even an hour on my knees before having been conscious to myself of having derived comfort, encouragement, humbling of the soul, etc., and often after having suffered much from wandering thoughts, for up to half an hour, I only then began to really pray.

I scarcely ever suffer in this way now, for my heart being brought into experimental fellowship with God, I speak to my Father about the things he has brought to me in his precious Word.

It often astonishes me that I did not sooner see this point (pp. 121–2).

Müller desired food for his soul, and he found it through meditation. Many others could provide a similar testimony.

Additional Note: Devotional Guides

From its beginnings in the sixteenth century, there has been a tradition within Protestantism of publishing Bibles which contain explanatory notes either in the margins or at the foot of the page. The first of these, and probably the most influential of all, was the *Geneva Bible* (1560). The notes were used both to help personal Bible study and to be read out in family prayers after the reading from Scripture and before the prayers.

Especially since the nineteenth century, Christians have
been encouraged to make use of what are usually called
"daily Bible-reading notes." These notes are now available from a great variety of sources and publishers. The
booklets come out once a quarter (or other regular periods) and contain directions to read a specific passage,
look at the notes and comments on it, and follow the directions for prayer. Much contemporary evangelical spirituality is formed by this practice, which is generally
followed in the so-called Quiet Time.

One real problem with the use of such notes is that the
user can so easily never learn the discipline of meditation.
He or she merely gets into the habit of receiving, as from
a spoon, predigested material, which, however good it is,
can never be as good for the individual soul as food which
one personally prepares and then actually eats. The heart
and will can never be driven by the same spiritual mo-
mentum from predigested food as they can by the very
inward act of spiritual digestion of the Word of God.

The leaders of the evangelical revival in the eighteenth
century (following the Reformers and the Puritans of earlier times) did not hesitate to give converts help in the
practice of meditation. The early Methodists, for example,
were given a tract called *The Large Minutes* which told
them how to search the Scriptures and to meditate on
their contents. Over the last two centuries, it would appear, evangelical leaders, revivalists, and evangelists have
given less and less advice on meditation. People indeed
still meditate, but they could be given more encouragement and help and spoon-fed much less.

6

The Counter-Reformation Way

Alongside the movement for revival and renewal which began around 1520 which we call the Protestant Reformation, there was a countermovement which sought to transform and revivify the part of the church in Europe which remained loyal to the pope (which we now call the Roman Catholic church). This Catholic movement, or Counter Reformation, included many outstanding and courageous men and women as well as some important new religious communities (e.g., the Jesuits).

Spain, always a loyal Catholic country where the Protestant Reformation made little headway, produced a rich spirituality (which is perhaps more influential now than it actually was in the late sixteenth century). Not only did Ignatius Loyola, founder of the Society of Jesus, come from Spain, but also St. Teresa (who wrote such books as *The Way of Perfection* and *The Mansions of the Interior Life*) and St. John of the Cross (who wrote *The Ascent of Mount Carmel, The Dark Night of the Soul,* and the *Living Flame of Love*) contributed as Discalced Carmelites to the spiritual strength of the Counter Reformation.

A friend of St. Teresa was St. Peter of Alcántara, founder of the Spanish Discalced Franciscans. He advised her when she made reforms within the Carmelite order, and he was much in demand as a spiritual counselor and director of

79

souls. His advice to laity and to novices in their first year within religious houses on meditation and prayer was set out in *Tratado de la oración y meditación* (Booklet on prayer and meditation) (1556). Apparently he was assisted in writing this tract by Louis de Granada (1504–1588), another Spanish writer on spirituality and author of *Libro de la oración y meditación* (a book which English Puritans knew and used). Whatever the precise origins of Peter's booklet, it is one of those short works of which we say that it is worth its weight in gold. In fact, the translation we shall use in this chapter is entitled *A Golden Treatise on Mental Prayer* (G. S. Hollings, ed. [New York: Morehouse-Gorham, 1905 reprint; Oxford: A. R. Mowbray, 1940]).

Before we examine the method of meditation proposed by St. Peter of Alcántara, it will be helpful to comment on the general understanding of the spiritual life which lies behind the writings of St. Teresa, St. John of the Cross, and St. Peter. Unless we see the general context in which meditation and prayer are set forth, we shall miss the real purpose of the method used.

It became increasingly common during the sixteenth century within the Counter Reformation to refer to the turning and converting to God from sin in terms of the threefold way (or the three ways)—the purgative, the illuminative, and the unitive ways. This process is to be compared with the Protestant concepts of justification and sanctification, where the latter includes the mortification of sin and the vivification of the soul. We should not think of the three ways as following each other in strict order. It is better to think of them as overlapping and, in part, running in parallel, as long as we remember that the purgative way is the beginning and the unitive way is the goal of the process of salvation from sin and into the joy of communion with God.

The *purgative way* is the way of penitence, of recognizing the reality of sin, its offensiveness to God, and the need for it to be cleansed and rejected. The *illuminative way* is the way of inner illumination by the Spirit, so that he brings into the soul his fruit of love, joy, peace, and faithfulness. In the light of the gospel the soul is also enabled to see what is pleasing to God. The *unitive way* is the way of spiritual union and communion with God: it is the way of love, wherein the love of God so fills the soul that it is united to God, who is Love. At some periods in the life of the Christian, the experience of the purgative way also includes that of the illuminative way, for there will be both a rejection of sin and a clear sight of what is pleasing to God. And at times the soul is simultaneously in both the illuminative and unitive ways, being guided by the Spirit as the love of God overflows into the soul.

Meditation is seen as belonging primarily to the experience of the purgative way but also as preparing the soul for the experience of the illuminative way. This view will become reasonably clear as we now look at the method of St. Peter.

The Method of Peter of Alcántara

I shall describe Peter's method objectively here. Then, in Appendix 1, I present two examples from the fourteen guided meditations which he supplies for beginners. At the end of the chapter, I shall show how his method fits into the purgative and illuminative ways and prepares the soul for the unitive way.

1. *Preparation.* "Before we enter upon the meditation, it is necessary to prepare the heart for this holy exercise, as one would tune a guitar for playing on it" (p. 86). Preparation includes taking up an appropriate bodily position, making the sign of the cross, seeking to bring one's thoughts under control, confessing our sins, asking for the illumination of the Holy Spirit, and praying to our Lord "that he may grant us grace to give ourselves up to this exercise with that attention and devotion, and with that

interior recollectedness and fear, and reverence, fitting for those who stand before the Divine Majesty" (p. 90).

2. *The reading.* Either Scripture or the devotional writings of a saint are to be read, in an attentive and serious manner.

> We should give to it not only our whole mind that we may fully understand what we read, but still more we should give to it our whole will that we may taste the sweetness of what we understand. And when we come upon some specially devout passage we should pause a little in it, for the better appreciation of its meaning. [p. 91]

It may be necessary to return to the reading later in the meditation or prayer to look again at a sentence or phrase.

3. *The meditation.* One kind of meditation uses primarily the imagination, and the other uses the understanding. The imaginative method will be used on the life, suffering, death, resurrection, ascension, and second coming of our Lord; the intellectual method will be used for such subjects as the attributes of God, his blessings to humankind, and the nature and forms of sin against him.

Concerning the use of imagination, Peter writes that "we should try to represent in our minds each item of our subject as it really is, or would become, and as though the action were being performed in our presence in the very place in which we are" (p. 92). With such a representation our reflections will be the more vivid and our feelings the keener. However, he warns against the use of too much violence in the exercise of the imagination; to get too involved in creating mental pictures will weary the mind, so that it is quite unable to pray.

The two examples in Appendix 1 illustrate these two kinds of meditation. Here it is necessary to emphasize some advice he gives concerning the general direction of meditation. It has special relevance to preachers, teachers, and theologians.

We should strive to avoid in this exercise any excessive intellectual speculation, and we should endeavour to treat the matter more with the affections and feelings of the will than with the discursive understanding. For without any doubt, those who set themselves down in prayer to meditate upon the Divine Mysteries, as though they were preparing themselves for preaching do not here hit upon the right way. For this mode of treating the subject is rather to dissipate, then to gather up the mind and to wander away from the subject rather than to penetrate within it. [p. 108]

The understanding is to direct the will toward God in love and worship, but the rational type of person will always face the temptation to consider the subject merely at the level of intellectual inquiry. In fact, little progress will be made in the discipline of meditation unless it is clearly recognized that the work of the intellect is to provide the heart and will with good reasons to desire and love God as the God of grace and glory.

4. *The thanksgiving.* We must first give thanks for the particular blessings on which we have been meditating, and then we are to extend the range of our thanks to God by recalling his blessings of creation, providence, and redemption. To recite a psalm such as Psalm 103 would be entirely appropriate.

5. *The offering or oblation of ourselves to God.* By this stage in our prayer/meditation we shall have a feeling much like that of the psalmist when he cried out, "How can I repay the LORD for all his goodness to me?" (116:12). Thus "we should offer ourselves to be his servants for ever, placing ourselves in his hands, giving up ourselves wholly to his will, that he may do with us whatever it shall please him to do, in time and eternity" (p. 96). Second,

We should offer to God the Father all the merits and labours of his divine Son, all the travails of his soul which, in his obedience, in this world he endured, from the man-

ger-crib to Calvary: for all these are our health, and the
inheritance which he bequeathed to us in that New Covenant by which he had made us heirs of so great a treas-
ure. [p. 97]

6. *The petition.* In the light of the offering/oblation
made, "We may confidently make our petition for gifts
and graces." He recommends petition for "zeal for the
honour of our Blessed Lord that all people and nations of
the world may know and praise and adore him," for the
whole church of God on earth, for the poor and sick, pris-
oners and captives, and for our own growth in the virtues,
graces, and fruit of the Holy Spirit.

He closes this section with a long and moving prayer
that we may truly love God with heart, soul, mind, and
strength all the days of our lives. In fact this prayer by
itself is a worthy subject for a meditation upon the love
of God.

Perhaps the most striking point about this method is
its completeness. It is not merely a method in meditation
but a way of prayer. Furthermore, it presents a path from
the purgative, through the illuminative, to the unitive
way to God, as the living God of holy, unquenchable love.
In a moment we shall see how he envisaged that a person,
arising from the prayer for the love of God, would enter
into the way of true contemplation, the unitive way.

Through the use of the written meditations on sin and
the Savior (see Appendix 1), we are intended to move well
into the purgative way, being both wholly conscious of,
and repentant for, our sins. Through further meditation
and prayer, we are intended to move into the joy of knowing God and of his provision for sinners in and through
Christ by the Holy Spirit within holy, mother church.
Thus we are into the illuminative way and moving under
the guidance of the Spirit and through our loving, disciplined endeavor toward the unitive way of contemplating

the glory of God and being overwhelmed by his eternal love.

Peter of Alcántara on Meditation and Contemplation

So that we fully understand the move from meditation to contemplation and from the illuminative toward the unitive way, Peter must actually speak fully for himself. Here is what he called his "chiefest counsel," or most important piece of advice to those using his method.

We should endeavour to unite Meditation with Contemplation, making of the one a ladder for attaining to the other. For this we must know that the very office of Meditation is to consider Divine things with studiousness and attention, passing from one to another, to move our hearts to some affection and deep feeling for them, which is as though one should strike a flint to draw forth from it the spark.

For Contemplation is to have drawn forth this spark: I mean, to have now found this affection and feeling which were sought for, and to be in peace and silence enjoying them; not with many discursive and intellectual speculations, but with simple gaze upon the truth.

Wherefore, saith a holy teacher, Meditation goes its way and brings forth fruit, with labour, but Contemplation bears fruit without labour. The one seeketh, the other findeth, the one consumeth the food, the other enjoys it; the one discourseth, and maketh reflections, the other is contented with a simple gaze upon the things, for it hath in possession their love and joy. Lastly, the one is as the means, the other as the end: the one as the road and journeying along it, the other as the end of the road and of the journeying.

From this is to be inferred a very common thing, which all masters of the spiritual life teach, although it is little understood of those who learn it; which is this, that, as the means cease when the end has been attained, as the voyaging is over when the port has been touched, so when, through the working out of our Meditation, we have come to the repose and sweet savour of Contemplation, we ought then to cease from that pious and laborious searching; and being satisfied with the simple gaze upon, and thought of, God—as though we had Him there present before us— we should rest in the enjoyment of that affection then given, whether it be of love, or of admiration, or joy, or other like sentiment.

The reason why this Counsel is given is this, that as the aim of this devotion is love and the affections of the will rather than the speculations of the understanding, when the will has been caught and taken by this affection, we should put away all those discursive and intellectual speculations, so far as we can, in order that our soul with all its forces may be fastened upon this affection without being diverted by the action of other influences. A learned teacher, therefore, counsels us that as soon as one should feel himself fired by the love of God, he should forthwith put aside all these considerations and thoughts—however exalted they may seem—not because they are really not good in themselves, but because they are then hindrances to what is better, and more important. For this is nothing else than that, having come to the end and purpose of our work, we should stay therein, and leave Meditation for the love of Contemplation. This may especially be done at the end of any exercise, that is, after the petition for the Divine love of which we have spoken, for one reason, because then it is supposed that the labour of the exercise we have just gone through has produced some Divine devotion and feeling, since, saith the wise man, "better is the end of prayer than the beginning" (cf. Eccles. vii. 8): and for another reason, that, after the work of Prayer and Meditation, it is well that one should give his mind a little rest, and allow it to repose in the arms of Contemplation. At this point, then, we should put away all other thoughts that may present themselves, and, quieting the mind and stilling the memory, fix all upon our Lord; and remembering that we are then in His Presence, no longer dwell upon the details of Divine things.

We should content ourselves with the knowledge which we have from Him by faith, and give to it our will and love, for this only is to embrace Him, and in this is the fruit of our whole Meditation. The understanding can apprehend little indeed of God, but the will can love Him much. Let us, then, retire within ourselves to the centre of our soul, where is now the Image of God, and there be intent upon Him; as one would listen to what He should say from some lofty tower, or as though we held Him within our hearts, and as if, in all the world, there were nothing save one's own soul and God Himself. And even of ourselves and of what we do we have to be forgetful for, as said one of the fathers of old, "That is the perfect prayer, when the one who is praying does not remember that he is praying." And not only at the end of the exercise, but in the midst of it, and at whatsoever other part of it, this spiritual swoon should come upon us, when the intellect is laid to sleep, we should make this pause and enjoy the blessing bestowed; and then, when we have finished the digestion of it, turn to the matter we have in hand, as the gardener does, when he waters his garden-bed; who, after giving it a sufficiency of water, holds back the stream, and lets it soak and spread itself through the depths of the earth; and then when this has somewhat dried up, he turns down upon it again the flow of water that it may receive still more, and be well irrigated.

But what the soul then feels, the light and satisfaction and charity it then enjoys, the peace it then receives, no words can tell, for this is the peace which passeth understanding, and the happiness which exceedeth all that this life can attain to. Some have been so taken captive by the love of God, that when they have hardly begun to think of it, the memory of this dear Name consumes them wholly. These have as little need of discourses and considerations to make them love Him, as the mother or the bride to delight themselves with the memory of son or husband, when any speak of them. And others there are who not only in the exercise of Prayer, but at other times, are so absorbed and saturated with the thoughts of God, as to forget all things, and their own selves for the sake of Him. For if the maddening fear of one who is lost could cause this oblivion, how much more should the love of that Infinite Beauty effect this, since grace could not be less powerful than nature and sin!

Whensoever, then, the soul should feel this, in whatsoever part of the Meditation it should be, we should on no account put the feeling aside; even if the whole time of the exercise should be spent upon it, without our bringing in and meditating upon the other subjects determined upon, unless these should be of obligation. For, as S. Augustine says, "We are to cease vocal Prayer, when at any time it should be a hindrance to devotion; and so, too, we should stay Meditation, when it would be a hindrance to Contemplation."

Hence, too, it is much to be observed, that as it may beho[o]ve us to cease Meditation at the call of spiritual affection, that we may rise up from the less to the greater; so, on the other hand, it may at times be right to leave affection for Meditation, as when through persevering in it, the excess of feeling might be dangerous to health. This is often the case with those who give themselves to these exercises, without advice, and being carried away by the force of Divine sweetness use them indiscreetly. In such a case as this, says a teacher, a good remedy is to stir up some responsive feeling by meditating for a while on the Passion of Christ, or on the sins and miseries of the world, in order to relieve the heart and set it at rest. [pp. 117–24]

Peter here describes what is often called the prayer of simplicity, or acquired contemplation, in contrast to infused contemplation (a special gift of grace given to some who have made much progress in the unitive way). We shall see that the Puritan emphasis upon meditation on the exalted Christ in heaven also could and did lead to this deeper form of union with God which Peter called contemplation, contemplative prayer, or the prayer of simplicity.

Those who wish to attempt this fine method of meditation and prayer need to bear in mind that it will take at least one hour in the morning or evening or both and that Peter believed it should be done following the morning and evening offices. It is difficult to see how it can be shortened or broken up without losing its movement toward its end—simple contemplation of God.

Additional Note: Mental Prayer

Perhaps it is now reasonably clear why Roman Catholics have so often referred to "mental prayer" instead of "meditation." They see meditation as a way of prayer which uses particularly the understanding and imagination. Yet its nature, as designed by God, is to lead to more prayer of a deeper kind. Thus Roman Catholics insist that meditation is not merely thinking, considering, or reflecting upon a biblical truth; it is also producing acts of love toward God and resolutions to live day by day as his true loving servant. Therefore it ought to lead to what is called affective and contemplative prayer.

Terminology can be confusing. It may be helpful to list the various grades or steps in prayer that were set forth in the Counter Reformation by St. Teresa and that have been widely accepted within the Roman Church. Four grades belong to the prayer which God calls all his children to offer to him, and a further five steps belong to the mystical prayer which God calls only a limited number to engage in and offer to him.

1. *Vocal prayer.* This prayer is offered to God by the congregation in divine worship or by an individual who prays aloud.

2. *Mental prayer.* This prayer involves a reasoned application of the mind to some supernatural truth in order to penetrate its meaning, to love it, and with God's help, to put it into practice. It leads on to acts of love to God and resolutions to do his will and be a channel of his love, which truly belong to the next stage of prayer.

3. *Affective prayer.* In this prayer the will predominates

and is the result of meditation, or mental prayer. It is the desiring to love and please God and the surrendering of the self to him.

4. *Prayer of simplicity.* This prayer may be called "acquired contemplation," "contemplative prayer," "the prayer of simple gaze," or "the simple vision of faith." It is the prayer of adoration in the sense that the whole soul (mind, heart, and will) is concentrated in the simple yet profound act of gazing upon, looking unto, and desiring God, as he is known through his self-revelation. Thus it is a prayer when the soul is still and quiet, for it is wholly absorbed by faith in the vision of God.

The next five stages belong to what is known as supernatural, or infused, contemplation, a state of prayer that God gives to some people who seek him with all their hearts. The steps are (5) infused contemplation, (6) the prayer of quiet, (7) the prayer of union, (8) the prayer of conforming union, and (9) the prayer of transforming union. In terms of the threefold way, these last four stages belong to the unitive way. See further, Jordan Aumann, *Spiritual Theology* (Huntington, Ind.: Our Sunday Visitor, 1980), chap. 12.

7

The Puritan Way

The Puritans were members of the Church of England in the seventeenth century who felt that, according to the Word of God, the recent Reformation had not gone far enough. They wanted to see the nation and the national, established church conform more closely to what they believed were the clear principles of Scripture. From 1600 to 1648, the Puritans were a party within the nation (within Parliament, at court, and in the church), but after the civil war one group of them, led by Oliver Cromwell, came to prominence and assumed power. In the 1650s plans were put in motion for the further reformation of the church.

The Protectorate collapsed, however, and the monarchy was restored in 1660, followed two years later by the restoration of the Church of England much as it had been before the civil war. Those who maintained their Puritan principles and felt unable to compromise either left for America (where thousands had already gone) or became Protestant Nonconformists outside the national church.

While the Puritan experiment failed in England, it was at first successful in New England, where the power of Puritan theology and practice lasted for over a century. In both England and New England, Puritan pastors set before their parishioners the high calling of being a justified and sanctified believer and the solemn duties of those who were the elect of God.

Meditation: A Means of Grace

For Puritans meditation was not an optional extra but was a duty by which all other duties were improved. As the oil lubricates the engine, so meditation facilitates and causes to be more useful such duties as repentance, faith, reading Scripture, prayer, loving God, and showing compassion.

Meditation began before adult regeneration and conversion to God. The unconverted were urged by Puritan pastors to repent of their sin and turn to God through Jesus Christ in saving faith. As preparation for genuine repentance, they were urged to meditate on their sinfulness before God. This requirement may be seen, for example, in the book *An Alarm to the Unconverted* (1671; Grand Rapids: Baker, reprint 1978), by Joseph Alleine. Among other requirements, he urged them to meditate "on the number of your sins . . . upon the aggravations of your sins, as they are the grand enemies of God and of your life . . . upon the desert of sin—it cries to heaven; it calls for vengeance . . . upon the deformity and defilement of sin." And he counseled, "O study your misery till your heart cry out for Christ as earnestly as ever a drowning man did for a boat, or the wounded for a surgeon."

Conversion was the door by which the believing sinner entered into the path of sanctification; it was the way of mortifying sin and allowing the new life created by the Spirit to become prominent and dominant. Within this process meditation was necessary as a means of obtaining and receiving the grace of God in Jesus Christ by the Holy Spirit. In the various "directories" (or guidebooks on how to live the Christian life) produced by Puritan pastors, meditation was described as a daily duty, together with prayer, Bible reading, and fulfilling one's Christian calling.

Apart from the daily fixed meditation, those in the way of sanctification were to use all available opportunities for occasional meditation. For example, rising from bed they were to think of the rising of Jesus from the dead; going to bed and wrapping themselves in the warm sheet could give rise to thoughts of the righteousness of Christ which encircled true believers; and as they walked down the lane through the trees, they could reflect upon God, Creator and Sustainer of the world.

Formal, sustained daily meditation best followed the careful and thoughtful reading of a passage of Scripture and was in turn best followed by fervent and sustained prayer. To read the Bible and not to meditate was seen as an unfruitful exercise: better to read one chapter and meditate afterward than to read several chapters and not to meditate. Likewise to meditate and not to pray was like preparing to run a race and never leaving the starting line. The three duties of reading Scripture, meditation, and prayer belonged together, and though each could be done occasionally on its own, as formal duties to God they were best done together.

In days of few late-night meetings and no telephones or televisions, the Puritans expected the faithful (except the sick, women with infant children, and young children) and especially pastors and heads of households to rise early and meet with the Lord before breakfast and the work of the day. This practice they believed was followed by the saints of the Bible and by Jesus himself.

Meditation on Sundays (or the Lord's Day, or the Sabbath) took a particular form. It was necessary as a preparation for attending worship, and it was required after hearing (and making notes on) the sermon. If the Lord's Supper was administered then, in order rightly to receive the sacrament, meditation on the Lord who was crucified for us was required before, during, and after the service. Such duties took time, and everyone was expected to share in them or at least show sympathy. It meant that Sunday

was not a day of fun but was a time of spiritual celebration, uplift, and nourishment for those who had the right
attitude. (For the unregenerate the Sabbath was boring
because, though there was rest from work, there were few
if any "worldly" pleasures available!)

Before we look at the actual method of formal meditation, it is necessary to recall that the Puritans located
the experience and practice of vital Christianity in what
they called "the affections" and that meditation was seen
as a divinely appointed way of stimulating or raising the
affections toward the glory of God. In the first chapter of
his great book *The Religious Affections* (1746), Jonathan
Edwards (one of the last of the New England Puritans)
defined the affections as "no other than the more vigorous
and sensible exercises of the inclination and will of the
soul." He further explained:

> God has endued the soul with two faculties: one is that
> by which it is capable of perception and speculation, or
> by which it discerns, and views, and judges of things;
> which is called the understanding. The other faculty is
> that by which the soul does not merely perceive and view
> things, but is some way inclined with respect to the things
> it views or considers; either is inclined *to* them, or is
> disinclined and averse *from* them; or is the faculty by
> which the soul does not behold things as an indifferent
> unaffected spectator, but either as liking or disliking,
> pleased or displeased, approving or rejecting (Carlisle,
> Pa.: Banner of Truth Trust, 1959, p. 24).

We know within our own hearts how we approve one
thing and reject another, loathe one thing and love another, are pleased with one thing and displeased with another. Sometimes our passions, feelings, desires, and hopes
are strong, and sometimes weak; they may vary from virtual indifference to great intensity.

The Puritans held that, since we are called "never [to]

be lacking in zeal ... [or] spiritual fervor" (Rom. 12:11) and to love God with our whole beings (Deut. 6:5), then the affections (love, desire, hope, joy, gratitude, and zeal, for example) were to be actively and intensely centered in the grace and glory of God. Vital Christianity means loving God, desiring to know him better and serve him more faithfully, hoping in and trusting in him as the Lord, rejoicing in his salvation, thanking and praising him for his mercies, and being zealous for his cause and kingdom.

Good sermons, it was often insisted, do not merely inform the mind with sound doctrine; they also stir up the affections, turning the will away from sin and toward the loving of God and one's neighbor. Like a good sermon, meditation also is a private means of raising, enlarging, and directing the affections through the reception and digestion of the Word of God in the heart from the mind. Thus it is clear why meditation best follows the attentive reading of the Bible and precedes fervent prayer.

We do not have to accept the Aristotelian psychology of the soul and its faculties (of mind, memory, intellect, and will) to follow and accept the general point made by Puritans concerning the affections. Christianity is obviously much more than the important matter of holding right belief. It involves loving God and serving him in his world in the name of Jesus Christ; thus it concerns trusting in him and desiring to see his will done in his world. It involves what we call the heart and will, as well as the mind (intellect and memory).

Since the Bible is filled with many noble themes, all interlocking one with another like the sections in a chain or the colors of the rainbow, the Puritans knew that the possible topics for meditation were many. They fully recognized, however, that certain themes were more important than others (e.g., the character of God, his law and his gospel, the person of Christ, and his death, resurrection, and exaltation into heaven) and ought to be more regularly the focus of meditation. The most important of

all themes for meditation was heaven—the place and
sphere where God is supremely known and worshiped
and enjoyed, where Christ is seated at the right hand of
the Father as our exalted King and Priest, and where the
saints truly rejoice with joy unspeakable and with a peace
that passes all understanding as they move from glory
into more glory.

Why did they insist on the primacy of God's heaven as
the supreme subject for meditation? First, because Christ
is there now and our salvation consists of union through
the Holy Spirit with him. He is our wisdom, righteousness, and sanctification. Second, we are pilgrims and sojourners on earth, journeying in faith, hope, and love
toward heaven in order to be with Christ there. Heaven
is the goal of our pilgrimage. And third, because we can
rightly live a Christian life in the present evil age only if
we have the mind of Christ, that is, if we are genuinely
heavenly minded, seeing our earth and this age in the
perspective of heaven. The Puritans did not despise this
world—their reforming zeal in social and political matters both in England and in New England shows that they
were very concerned about this world. Rather, they believed that God in Christ, the center of heaven, ought to
be the center of all our faith, hope, and love. It seems to
me that the Puritans were right, and for this reason I
wrote my *Longing for the Heavenly Realm* (London: Hodder and Stoughton, 1986), inspired by some of their own
published meditations on heaven and the glory of Christ.

Appendix 2 is an extract from chapter 13 of Richard
Baxter's *Saints' Everlasting Rest*, in which, after stating
the doctrine of the rest (i.e., being in heaven with Christ)
in earlier chapters, he begins to show that only by the
duty of meditation will believers actually long for and
desire this great gift of God. (See the bibliography at
the end of this chapter for further Puritan works on
meditation.)

The Method of Meditation

Now we turn to the method used by many Puritans. Since formal, stated meditation was always seen as an individual, not a group, experience, I shall describe it in brief, using the first person singular as though I were a Puritan.

1. *Preparation.* Having risen early, I find a suitable place in the home where I can both sit comfortably and kneel conveniently and where I am unlikely to be disturbed. I recall that God invites me to come to him by the merits and mediation of his beloved Son, my Savior, Jesus Christ. In his name I seek the Lord.

2. *Bible reading.* I continue my reading of the Minor Prophets. Today I come to Habakkuk, which has only three chapters. Praying for God's illumination of my mind and heart, I read it all carefully. The prophet is dealing with the moral problem of how God, who is righteous, can be raising up and using the Chaldeans, who are wicked and cruel, to inflict his judgment upon his covenant people, Judah.

3. *Choice of theme.* In the last few verses of chapter 3, the prophet solves the moral problem by his statement of total faith. I find these verses so moving that I take them for my meditation.

> Though the fig tree does not bud
>   and there are no grapes on the vines,
> though the olive crop fails
>   and the fields produce no food,
> though there are no sheep in the pen
>   and no cattle in the stalls,
> yet I will rejoice in the LORD,
>   I will be joyful in God my Savior.
>
> [vv. 17–18]

4. *Consideration.* I want to have a faith, trust, and joy like that of Habakkuk. And the Bible supplies me with

many reasons why I ought to have—and can have—such a faith. I recall first that the harvest of the trees and fields is the free gift of God to us. He can cause the harvest to be plentiful or minimal, to be abundant or to fail. Second, as an undeserving sinner I have no automatic or inherent right to expect a good harvest or to enjoy any other blessings of the created order. If I do have them, it is by the goodness and mercy of God; if I do not, then it is because God in his providence has decided that it will be so. This arrangement I must believe and accept. Third, in his covenant of grace made with me and for me in Jesus Christ, my Lord, God tells me that I can never be separated from his love, that, whatever my external circumstances, I cannot be removed from his protection and blessing. Lord, I believe this promise—but help my unbelief! Fourth, there is much for me to rejoice about. My God is the Creator and Judge of the universe. In Jesus he has provided me with salvation, and he promises to bring me to the full enjoyment of eternal life. I shall rejoice and be glad, for I know that the Lord God is for me. Finally, Jesus, for the joy that was set before him, endured the cross and all its shame. O God, fill me with the joy of Jesus!

5. *Soliloquies.* As I consider, I also talk to myself silently within. "O my soul, whatever be my external circumstances at any time and in any place, you must always believe that God is the Lord and that he will preserve and keep you." "Be joyful, O my soul, for God has given to you so many rich and wonderful promises to bless, preserve, keep, and support you for the sake of Jesus." "I shall trust and rejoice in the LORD, for there are many excellent reasons why I should do so and not one good one why I should not rejoice!"

6. *Imagination.* I also picture the prophet in my mind's eye. I see him among barren fig trees, empty vines, and olive trees; I see him in the desolate fields; I see him in the empty pens and stalls. Yet I see on his bearded face signs not of anger and anxiety but of radiant peace and

joy. In all his troubles he is trusting in the Lord. O my God, give me a joy, peace, and trust like his.

7. *Prayer.* Falling upon my knees, I continue in prayer, adoring God, who is entirely and wholly trustworthy and worthy of our worship. I confess my lack of trust, joy, and peace. I pray that the church will be obedient to God's call and not need to feel his chastisement. I ask God's blessing on my family.

8. *Resolve.* I leave my devotions in order to lead the family prayers and with the resolve to recall continually throughout the day the message of God to me through Habakkuk.

The Use of Imagination in Meditation

In the description of method I included the use of the imagination because the majority of Puritan writers, in agreement with those of the Catholic Counter Reformation, commend its careful use. In *The Saints' Everlasting Rest*, for example, Richard Baxter encourages the meditator, on the basis of Revelation 21–22 and other passages, to imagine the heavenly Jerusalem and to compare its excellence with the best that can be experienced on earth. He invites people to take a walk around the celestial city to see its glories and to feel its loving warmth. While he does not go as far as Ignatius Loyola, who invites people to use all their five senses (including taste and smell) to imagine the heavenly city, Baxter certainly is uninhibited in commending the use of the imagination controlled by the images and pictures of Holy Scripture.

In later Puritanism, however, an insistence developed that meditation should not include the use of imagination but should make use only of "rational consideration" as prompted by the Holy Spirit and the exercise of faith. A major protagonist and defender of this position was John Owen (1616–1683) in his massive *Discourse Concerning the Holy Spirit* (1674). Owen was a purist and, in my judgment, overstressed the supernatural work of the Spirit by not making sufficient room for the genuine and earnest strivings after holiness of ordinary, faithful believers. I think that Baxter was a better pastor with a more realistic understanding of what ordinary believers needed in order to digest and obey the written Word of God.

We know from daily experience that the imagination enables us (1) to bring home to ourselves the reality of an experience of the past, whether memorable or sad, important or ordinary; (2) to grasp with more intensity some experience of the moment (e.g., how another person feels or what an object looks like, having heard only a description of it); and (3) to taste beforehand an event yet to be experienced (e.g., a birthday treat or success in examinations). Though it is essentially realistic, it can transform itself into fancy and so it has to be used under the control of our reason.

The major use of imagination by the Catholic writers on meditation is to picture the arrest, trial, crucifixion, and resurrection of our Lord to deepen our love for him and to make us eager to serve him. But when the passage for meditation is taken from one of the Gospels, we of course can imagine Jesus in a variety of situations, so that we can, as it were, hear his word and witness his action and so become obedient to his word and call.

All of us possess this capacity to a greater or less degree. Some of us have a highly pictorial imagination and can represent before our eyes a very clear picture. Others have a great sense of identifying with the feelings of others and representing these to our minds. We must learn to know ourselves in order to use this capacity beneficially to raise our desires for God and communion with him. Furthermore, the more we actually know the contents of the Bible (aided by careful use of dictionaries, pictures, photos, and maps), the more we are able rightly to use our imagination in the service of our Lord as we draw closer to him.

Bibliography

Alleine, Richard. *Vindiciae Pietatis* (1663).
Ball, John. *Treatise of Divine Meditation* (1650).
Baxter, Richard. *The Saints' Everlasting Rest* (1650).
Calamy, Edmund. *The Art of Meditation* (1667).
Culverwell, Ezekiel. *Time Well Spent in Sacred Meditation* (1634).
Fenner, William. "The Use and Benefit of Divine Meditation." In *Works*
    (1657).
Flavell, John. *Navigation Spiritualized* (1663).
————. *Husbandry Spiritualized* (1669).
————. *The Mystery of Providence* (1678).
Owen, John. *Meditations and Discourses on the Glory of Christ* (1684).
Ranew, Nathaniel. *Solitude Improved by Divine Meditation* (1670).
Reynolds, Edward. *Meditations on the Holy Sacrament of the Lord's
    Supper* (1639).
Sibbes, Richard. *Divine Meditation and Holy Contemplation* (1638).
White, Thomas. *A Method and Instructions for the Art of Divine Med-
    itation* (1655).

To these works should be added such writings of John Bunyan as *The Pilgrim's Progress* and *Grace Abounding to the Chief of Sinners.* They are the written record of meditation upon the Christian life and upon Bunyan's own conversion.

8

Learning Meditation Together

Ever since the sixteenth century, Roman Catholics have promoted retreats, or periods away from the normal course of things, that are aimed at finding the presence of God in silence and prayer, meditation and contemplation. Retreats were originally for the religious—monks and nuns, bishops and priests—but the laity were soon provided for as well.

Retreats began in the Anglican communion through the influence of the Oxford (Anglo-Catholic) movement of the nineteenth century, but they became common only in this century, more especially since the Second World War. Now they seem to be used by Protestants of many kinds, their Roman Catholic origin being forgotten. A biblical justification is usually sought in such a passage as Mark 6:30–31. "The apostles gathered around Jesus and reported to him all they had done and taught. Then, because so many people were coming and going that they did not even have a chance to eat, he said to them, 'Come with me by yourselves to a quiet place and get some rest.' "

The attraction of retreats is not only in getting away from the telephone, the pressures, and the busyness. It is also in being alongside others on the same spiritual pilgrimage and in being in the presence of a teacher or leader who from his or her own experience and knowledge of the

103

tradition, can show the way of prayer and meditation, of contemplation and adoration. Many people today are finding great help in their Christian commitment by going on retreats.

People also testify to gaining help and encouragement in meditation and prayer through membership in small groups which meet weekly or biweekly in order to practice meditation together and then to engage in contemplative prayer. Here I refer to the adoring and loving of God by mind, heart, and will in a simple, yet profound way. The way of group meditation is not, of course, a substitute for individual meditation but rather an aid and inspiration to it.

Some Christian groups who seek to meditate and pray together have probably been influenced either directly or indirectly by people who themselves have been influenced by Eastern methods of meditation. Thomas Merton, for example, became increasingly fascinated toward the end of his life by the methods and goals of Buddhists as they engaged in meditation. I cannot evaluate this influence here, but I fear that it can become too strong and lead to the virtual abandonment of classic Western meditation—the fixing of the mind on revealed Christian truth in order to warm the heart in its loving of God and neighbor. Yet I also see that we in the West can learn much from Eastern cultures concerning the use of silence, bodily posture in prayer, and ascetic practices. It is an area where we need to proceed with care, remembering that our goal is to draw near to the living God as he is revealed and made known to us in Jesus Christ, who is the Way, the Truth, and the Life.

In this chapter we shall examine two methods of group meditation and end by making some practical comments on the value of each method. The first shows little or no influence of Eastern concepts and practice, while the second acknowledges its debt to such influence.

Coulson's Method of Group Meditation

The Anglican Fellowship of Contemplative Prayer, founded in 1946, owes its approach to meditation and prayer to Robert Coulson (b. 1899), author of *The Way into God* (London: John Murray, 1948), *Into God* (1956), and *The Threefold Reality* (1960). It currently has small groups meeting in various provinces of the Anglican communion; their practice is to go on retreat together each year.

The basic method used by these groups is found in Coulson's book *Into God* and is set forth in an abbreviated form in the booklet *Towards Contemplation* (1977) by Peter Dodson and in a small publication of the fellowship entitled *On Course in Contemplation* (1980). Those who belong to the groups are usually High Church individuals who put great emphasis on reception of Holy Communion at the Sunday Eucharist. This approach is not for those of little interest or commitment. Rather, it is for those who recognize that something is fundamentally wrong with Western society in its increasingly obvious moving away from the possibility of spiritual union with God in Christ Jesus. They must be ready to make a determined effort to reverse this trend both in themselves and in society itself. Finally, it is for those who feel a certain intensity in their need for God, as God, and a longing for fellowship with him.

Coulson's foundational belief is the traditional, classic doctrine of the living God as triune, who made human beings in his image and for fellowship with him. By their own rebellion human beings have placed themselves in a state of alienation from God and thus need to be reconciled to him. The gospel of God concerning Jesus Christ is the good news of the possibility of reconciliation and salvation. God, the Lord, the ultimate I Am (Exod. 3:14), has made a way in and through his incarnate Son, Jesus Christ (who is also I Am—John 8:58), for each individual human being to return into union with himself.

In the return to God, the human need for union with God is satisfied in three main stages. First, the mind comes into play: the need and the possibilities of satisfying it are known (cognized). Then the heart becomes involved: the feelings (affections) are aroused in the form of desires or aversions. Last, the will is set in motion; the striving (conation) commences to satisfy the desires or aversions. Coulson remarks that "the enormous proliferation of sterile theological speculation alone gives one some notion of the numbers of seekers who have become bogged down in studying the Way into God without actually entering upon it" (*Into God*, p. 29). The method, as we shall see, is related to these three stages.

Though the return to God in Christ is for each individual to travel in, he or she ought not to travel alone. God is the one and only I Am, but there are millions of "I ams." Human beings in search of God through Jesus are bound together in him, and so they ought to help each other into and along the Way—thus the need for meeting in a small group and going together in retreat and fully participating in the Sunday Eucharist.

Finally, in the actual practice of meditation only the words of God spoken directly by a prophet or by the Lord Jesus himself are actually used. The rest of the scriptural revelation is not discounted but is there to provide the general context and teaching. The clear and direct (as they may be called) utterances of God to humankind are used because of their immediate efficacy and clarity.

Inspired by attending a group meeting at least once a month and by going on an annual retreat, an individual pursues the method alone (preferably) twice daily—in the morning after dressing and in the evening before the meal. He or she brings to it the knowledge, experience, and spirituality gained through participation in corporate worship, sacramental reception, and the traditions and teaching of the church, as a member of a local parish congregation.

The method is much the same whether it be practiced alone or together. It provides the mind, heart, and will with the opportunity and the reasons to draw nearer to God in the body of Christ and to receive his grace. To complete one cycle of the basic method takes six months, and Coulson held that beginners needed to go through the cycle four times before they could really claim to be into the way of meditation and contemplative prayer. The following subjects were to be taken in turn, each for one month: divine peace, divine joy, divine all-power, divine wisdom, divine love, and divine truth.

It seems that few actually do follow this procedure so rigidly, since in the busyness of our culture there is a desire to have results rather more quickly than after two years. Yet, Coulson's approach is profound (and a mere summary here does not do justice to his reasoning) and is worthy of being taken very seriously.

Here in brief is what he recommended:

1. *Position.* The best position is not kneeling but sitting. Both feet should be on the ground, the knees comfortably apart, the hands resting lightly on the knees. The head and back should as far as possible be in a straight line. The body should be relaxed but not slumped.

2. *The invitation.* The invitation of Jesus is to be recalled: "Come to me, all you who are weary and burdened, and I will give you rest" (Matt. 11:28). Then our burdens, problems, and difficulties are to be brought to him, and we are to accept his *rest*. This coming is not to be rushed; maintain silence for two minutes.

3. *God's word in the mind.* This month the living word of God is the word of peace. Before the beginning of meditation we shall have ascertained in study what God's peace truly is—not merely the cessation of conflict but the positive presence of God himself, radiating warmth, belonging, light, and hope within us. We use the words of Jesus, which we say slowly over and over again in the mind, concentrating on each part and letting them enter

into the very depths of the mind. He said, "Peace I leave with you; my peace I give you. I do not give to you as the world gives. Do not let your hearts be troubled and do not be afraid" (John 14:27).

4. *God's Word in the heart.* As Paul urged the Colossian Christians, "Let the peace of Christ rule your hearts" as you "let the word of Christ dwell in you richly" (3:15–16). Continuing in silence, slowly repeating to ourselves the words of Jesus, we find that they begin to warm our hearts and to bring us some sense of what God's peace actually is.

5. *The giving of thanks.* After five or more minutes of silent appropriation of the Word of God, which contains and brings the peace of God, we pray in words such as these, "We thank Thee, O Lord, for Thy Peace. And we offer and present unto Thee, as far as we are able, all that we are, all that we do, and all that we have."

6. *God's Word in the will.* In meditation we moved from a *notion about* peace to an *experience of* peace. Going into "the world," we now must exercise our wills in such a way that they know this peace. To do this Coulson suggests that we create a watchword based on the words of Christ we have been repeating (e.g., "divine peace" or "Christ's peace" or "my peace") and say it to ourselves at every opportunity during the day, especially when anxiety or resentment or problems arise. Such a simple method provides an opportunity for the peace of God to fill our souls. This watchword ought especially to be used as we arise in the morning and as we go to bed for sleep.

This method of monthly themes must obviously be supplemented by other devotions such as the office of morning and evening prayer and by intercession. In praying for others we are able to direct our wills in such a manner that we effectively pray that God's peace, the peace of the Lord Jesus, enter their hearts. In this way there is a real connection between the meditation and intercession.

Coulson gave specific advice to the priests whom he

calls "Witnesses to the Word," or conductors of retreats. He insists that a retreat conductor is there as a witness and not as a director. His witness to the Word of God, the great I Am, is seen primarily in the introductory talks he gives before each session of silence/prayer in the chapel. In these he is to avoid repeating the views of this or that person and instead to concentrate on setting forth the word of Jesus. He must not allow his witnessing to become a sermon or a lecture.

The witness may, however, make use of carefully stated personal testimony concerning how he has received in mind, heart, and will the words that he is witnessing to and sharing with the retreatants. Finally, he should keep to the traditional shape of three twenty-minute sessions in the hour. The first talk aims at preparing the mind to receive the Word and best consists of a theological exposition of the words chosen. Then comes the silence in which each person mentally repeats the words (e.g., "I am the Way, the Truth, and the Life"), digesting their content and meaning.

The second talk, beginning twenty minutes after the first, again lasts for no more than ten minutes. Its content best consists of an account by the witness himself of how he has experienced the power and significance of this Word. Then follows the second silence, in which all seek to allow the power of the Word to inflame their hearts and direct their desires toward God.

The third talk aims at preparing the will to receive the Word and to act in the light of it (i.e., to put theology into practice). This result can be accomplished by giving an example of how the Word is to be applied in personal terms in, say, a difficult situation and also by guiding the retreatants in intercessory prayer, asking that the Word enter the people prayed for and be like good seed in fertile hearts.

This sequence is repeated several times during a retreat, the rest of the time being spent in reading, quiet walks, and so on. This method works best when those using it are at the same time growing deeper into knowledge of the Bible and of the devotional heritage of the church. Only with this rich experience can they truly benefit from the silence, for they are able to set the Word in a viable and dynamic context and so truly digest it in the heart.

Main's Method of Group Meditation

This method is associated with the name of John Main, a Roman Catholic monk. In 1954 Main was taught a very simple method of meditation in Malaya by an Indian teacher. He repeated his mantra (a Christian phrase) continually for half an hour, morning and evening. Later he became a monk in the Roman Catholic church and was surprised and distressed to find that he was required to drop his Eastern method and adopt the Western style developed in the Counter Reformation.

Later he read the writings of John Cassian (c. 360–435) known as the "Conferences," which are descriptions of monastic life based on his own experiences with the monks of the deserts of Egypt. Main was overjoyed to discover that Cassian employed a method of prayer without ceasing which he took to be of much the same kind as the method of meditation taught by his Indian teacher. In fact, Main was guilty of oversimplification.[1]

1. John Cassian certainly made a discovery that, through continual repetition of a scriptural verse, that verse usually remains evocative. Being a man whose piety was deeply embedded in the Psalter, he took as his own favorite verse for constant repetition Psalm 70:1, "Hasten, O God, to save me; O Lord, come quickly to help me." In Conference 10, in a passage of great beauty and devotional power, he reveals just how this prayer was for him an unceasing prayer. But he also used other verses to be the basis for a life of prayer between the times of corporate prayer with other monks at set times of the day and night. Though his constantly repeated prayer could trigger meditation at any time, it was not meant to be repeated in the way in which Main learned from his Indian teacher. Furthermore, Cassian did accept the need for both the reading (and hearing) of Scripture and its mem-

After a short stay at Thomas Merton's hermitage, he began what he believed was his life's mission: to teach meditation in the way he had learned it in Malaya and found it in the writings of John Cassian. Books by John Main include *Word into Silence* (London: Darton, Longman & Todd, 1981), *Letters from the Heart* (1982), *Moment of Christ* (1984), and *The Present Christ* (1985). His method is used at the Benedictine Priory of Montreal, Canada, the Christian Meditation Centre in London, and by small groups in many places.

The method of meditation is apparently very simple.

> Sit down. Sit still and upright. Close your eyes tightly. Sit relaxed but alert. Silently, interiorly begin to say a single word. We recommend the prayer-phrase, "Maranatha." Recite it as four syllables of equal length. Listen to it as you say it, gently but continuously. Do not think or imagine anything—spiritual or otherwise. If thoughts and images come, these are distractions at the time of meditation, so keep returning to simply saying the word. Meditate each morning and evening for between twenty and thirty minutes (*Light Within*, London: L. T. Darton, 1986, p. xii)

Though simple, it is obviously demanding of time and commitment.

The term *Maranatha* (an Aramaic prayer meaning "our Lord, come," used in 1 Cor. 16:22 and in the *Didache*, 10:6) is known as the mantra. Other such phrases are used, but this one is the most popular, especially for beginners. Besides the daily requirement of two periods of meditation, those who seek this path of inner meditation are urged to

orization. And he expected that monks would meditate upon (in the sense of consider and reflect on) this Scripture and also call it to mind during the day as they did their manual labor or as they awoke in the night. See further John Cassian, *Conferences*, trans. Colm Luibheid, with an introduction by Owen Chadwick (New York: Paulist Press, 1985); Owen Chadwick, *John Cassian* (Cambridge University Press, 1968).

join a group which meets each week. At a group the usual format is to hear a talk on an aspect of meditation and then to spend twenty or so minutes together in silence, each member repeating the mantra silently. The general philosophy is that saying the word enables individuals to enter into an ever profounder inner silence in which they not only can discover their true self but also allow God to be who he is within the soul. To achieve this silence all intellectual and imaginative activity of mind has to be banished. All great or trivial thoughts have to be allowed to disappear. The mantra alone must be said.

In his enthusiastic commendation of this method in *Light Within*, Laurence Freeman, osB, claims many spiritual benefits for those who, maintaining their commitment to Christ in regular worship, also practice this form of meditation twice a day. He enumerates the following benefits:

> By silence of mind and spirit we are brought to that point of irreducible truth when we not only find ourselves but lose ourselves. (p. 7; ref. to Mark 8:35–36)

> Repetition purifies. The mantra will purify your heart, your consciousness, and bring you to that pure simplicity of a child, which we need if we are to enter the kingdom. (p. 13; ref. to Mark 10:14–15)

> Saying our word faithfully, simply and lovingly, brings us to that stillness where we see the light clearly both within and around us. (p. 15; based on Ps. 36:9, "in your light we see light")

> The moral reality of our life begins to mature because we are impelled to be truthful to the implications of saying the mantra in every level of life. (p. 19)

> What is happening is that we are being unified, which means that the different dimensions of our being are gradually being brought into synchrony, into harmony, into step with each other. (p. 27)

Every time we meditate we undergo *renewal*, which is another word to describe in the New Testament that experience of transformation, shedding old-ness and being made new. (p. 31)

It is not claimed, however, that these and other benefits are instantaneous. They may come slowly or quickly, sooner or later. The important thing is to persevere joyfully with the saying of the mantra.

As we have already noted, John Main claimed that his method was much the same as that of John Cassian. Another claim made within the movement is that the method is similar to the Greek and Russian Orthodox method of continually saying the Jesus Prayer ("Lord Jesus Christ, Son of God, have mercy upon me a sinner"). Usually, however, those who do say the Jesus Prayer are not asked to negate their powers of intellect and imagination. Yet another claim is that the method is much the same as that set forth in the anonymous *Cloud of Unknowing*. The teaching of this important book is that God lies beyond the cloud of darkness and unknowing and therefore the human will alone can attempt to pierce the cloud with its naked impulse of love. It is a book about the way to, and the practice of, contemplation—union with God. Only in a very general way does it bear comparison with John Main's method.

The old saying, "The proof of the pudding is in the eating," perhaps applies here. A growing number of people are claiming to have deepened their Christian experience and commitment and achieved greater peace and inner harmony by using Main's method. However, unless it is rooted deeply and thoroughly in the Christian tradition of corporate worship and orthodox teaching, it will be no better or worse than the various forms of Eastern meditation that have been offered to us by a variety of gurus.

Many churches have house groups and small Bible study and prayer fellowship groups. It would seem to be quite easy, with general consent, for those to become groups where people actually learn the practice of meditation. After the reading of Scripture, there could be guided meditation with periods of silence, leading to a time of intercession. Any one of the individual or group methods could be adapted for such a purpose. Certainly many people who wish to meditate privately would like to be helped by belonging to a warm fellowship which itself practices meditation.

Epilogue

The Effects of Meditation

Throughout this book I have been insisting on the great value of meditation as a means of training the soul and of drawing near to God. When rightly pursued it has four particular effects in the interior life of the meditator.

First of all, *meditation enlightens the understanding.* Roman Catholic writers formerly spoke of meditation as "discursive prayer" because the reason is busy running about within the themes of Scripture to seek fresh light upon the subject in view. The knowledge being sought by the understanding is not knowledge of an abstract system but of a *personal* God. Thus the understanding is that of how the Lord relates to us as his creation and how we are called by him to relate to him; the knowledge we gain is intuitive and by faith.

Meditation is not a time for sharpening the critical faculty and engaging in theological speculation or seeking to solve intellectual problems. It is not a time for the study of theology! It is a chewing of the cud rather than a searching for new food. It is understanding God in order to love and serve him, and so it is a waiting on him as the King of Kings. (I fear that many students and teachers of theology miss out on scriptural meditation because they allow the attractive content of doctrines and philosophies

115

to fill their minds and never come to understanding *in order to* know, or have communion with, God.)

In the second place, *meditation purifies the imagination.* As we learn to imagine the various parts of the life and ministry of our Lord, to see him before Pilate and on the cross, to encounter him as the resurrected Lord, and to meet him on the way to Emmaus, we allow the Holy Spirit both to raise our desires and to cleanse our imagination. As we see in our mind's eye the glory of heaven through the apocalyptic symbolism provided in parts of the Bible, we increase our longing to enter that heavenly realm to join those who are pure in heart. As we feel the joy of the disciples at Pentecost as they were filled with the Spirit and longed to testify for their heavenly Lord, so we too have the desire to be temples of the same Spirit and be led and guided by him, as he is the Spirit of Christ.

In the third place, *meditation kindles the heart so that it is aflame with the love of God.* We recall that the first commandment is that we are to love God with our hearts—indeed, with our whole beings. As we consider the revelation of God in Jesus Christ, as we imagine what pain he suffered for our sake and what love took him to the cross, as we see the changed lives of his disciples when he rose from the dead, when we imagine those vast depths of love that are in God's own being, and when we recognize that we are called to love others as Christ loved us, then little by little our hearts begin to glow with devotion. There is no massive change overnight for most people, but over a long period, we find that the love of God is setting our hearts on fire with zeal for his glory and love of his name and will. This state is not emotionalism, but it is the emotional nature being filled with the right kind of desires and affections. Unless our hearts become the place where the love of God can dwell, then we have no real Christianity, even though we may know much theology and be faithful churchgoers (1 Cor. 13).

Finally, *meditation inspires the will.* The final test of

love is action. "Love your neighbor as yourself"; "love each other as I have loved you" (Mark 12:31; John 15:12). Again, the meditator cannot expect to be a totally changed person, losing all hesitancy, inhibition, and lack of motive to love the neighbor, within a day or two. The strengthening of the will, in its resolve and commitment to doing God's will practically in real-life situations, is a gradual process. However, like putting dry wood on fire, the action of the will does increase the love of God in the heart and makes the next action of love that much easier. In fact, we can see the whole process through the imagery of a fire. It is kindled originally by the work of the mind (understanding, memory, and imagination), it leaps up in flames as desires for God and his glory and love of him and his name are created, and it is then kept burning both by acts of love and by further meditation.

It all sounds easy. In practice it is tough going, especially at first until habits of life are established in which it fits without too much discomfort and dislodgement. Surely we cannot afford not to try!

We have surveyed the biblical teaching on meditation; we have examined various methods of meditation and have noticed that each of them aims at directing the soul toward loving, trusting, and obeying God. The Christian who does not meditate is keeping closed an important channel both of being drawn closer to God and of drawing closer to him. There are, thus, sound reasons why we ought to make space and time for meditation and why, to get us started, we ought to join a group, go on retreat, or be advised by someone who has already traveled on this road. When both the Roman Catholic and the Protestant (not to mention the Eastern Orthodox) traditions agree in recommending a form of spirituality, then only the foolish will discount that advice.

In the rest of this Epilogue, I set out another method of meditation which I might call "An Anglican Approach," since I am a priest of the Church of England. It is adaptable for group meditation and can be used in any Christian denomination.

An Approach to Meditation

This method is designed and intended for those who regularly attend corporate worship on Sundays and who desire to know God and draw near to him every day of their lives. It also assumes that we can make the space and time for not less than twenty minutes each day and that we are following some fixed system of daily Bible readings (e.g., a lectionary). The meditation is best done in the morning after dressing but before eating. I realize that in certain homes to find peace and quiet is not easy. Where there is a will, however, there is a way.

The method may be described as follows, using the first person singular throughout.

1. *Preparation.* This step includes both physical and spiritual preparation. I must make sure I am in a comfortable position. If I kneel or sit, I must ensure that my spine is straight and my head is also straight. I take a few deep breaths in order to relax my body.

As I prepare physically I also recall the presence of God with me and around me. Wherever I am in his universe, he is near to me. As his adopted child by grace, I also know that the Spirit of Christ is within me because I am a member of the body of Christ. Using my imagination I see Jesus. In the first place I see him sitting on a rock teaching his disciples and I put myself among them. Secondly, I see him appearing in his resurrection body to his disciples and saying "Peace!" to them; again I see myself with them.

2. *Bible reading.* I read the lesson(s) listed in the lectionary. Today the New Testament reading is that for the Wednesday of the eighth week before Christmas and is Matthew 5:21–26. I picture Jesus on the mountainside

saying these words to his assembled disciples, whom I join.

3. *Prayer for illumination and help.* Both before reading and after reading I pray silently that the Holy Spirit will bring to my mind the understanding and meaning that is in the mind of Christ himself.

4. *Theme.* To use every part of the reading for meditation will take too long, so I choose one of its themes: *God, who is my Judge, not only sees my actions but knows my thoughts, feelings, and attitudes.* (This thought is based on vv. 21–22; I could have taken the theme of reconciliation from vv. 23–26.)

5. *Exercise of memory.* To initiate meditation (without the bother of referring to books), I need to recall what I know concerning God and myself. I remember teaching such as the following:

> My inner self (my mind, heart, and will) is seriously affected by sin. Jesus said that out of the heart comes forth a great variety of sinful thoughts and deeds. For this reason I am sometimes angry.

> God has graciously placed within me his Spirit—the Spirit who indwelt and indwells Jesus Christ—who is always ready to sanctify, strengthen, and guide me.

> God calls me to love him and to love my neighbor.

> At the end of my life or the end of the age I shall appear before the judgment seat of Christ to give an account of my thoughts and deeds.

This kind of recalling fills out my chosen theme.

6. *Consideration.* To deepen meditation I now must ask, with special reference to the theme, the following questions. What does it tell me about my Lord, God's church, myself, and the world? (Not all these questions will be always relevant, but it is well to keep them in mind.) First, it tells me not only that my God is nearer to me than my own breathing but that he knows more about me than I

know about myself. Thus I cannot keep anything from
him. I cannot hide any secret from him. He sees the anger
in my heart. Then, it tells me that the church is to be a
community which is aware that God's call to holiness and
perfection applies both to the inner and outer life, to heart,
motives, will, and action. So I need to pray both for purity
of heart and integrity of character for myself and others.
Third, it calls me to be watchful over my thoughts and
attitudes as well as my deeds. I must be alert for temptation from the world, the flesh, and the devil. Certainly
I must avoid anger as well as murdering a person's character by ill-chosen or incorrect words. Finally, it presents
me with the reality of a world made up of people whose
hearts are sinful and who therefore need God's forgiveness, cleansing, and salvation. I thus need to take every
opportunity to commend the gospel of Jesus Christ by
word and example.

7. *Imagination.* I seek to see myself as a changed person—as being the kind of person that God wants me to
be. (Some themes are more easily developed than others
in the imagination; e.g., Jesus before Pilate or Jesus carrying his cross to Golgotha.) I desire and long to be such
a person.

8. *Prayer.* The Word of God has warmed, challenged,
and directed my mind and heart. From what I have seen,
understood, and felt, I now pray,

> confessing my sins and praying for cleansing
>
> praising God for his all-pervasive and omnipresent
> Spirit
>
> thanking God because he is not only my Maker and
> Judge but also my Savior in Christ Jesus
>
> asking for strength to overcome temptation and to keep
> my heart and mind filled with pure and uplifting
> thoughts
>
> and interceding for the congregation to which I belong.

9. *Resolutions.* To go forth on my daily routine I resolve to take with me, and often to repeat, a phrase, word, or sentence from my meditation. "God not only knows me thoroughly; he also will help me everywhere and always."

No method ought to be followed slavishly or rigidly. If I find that as I proceed I am drawn by the magnet of divine light and love into contemplation of God with singleness of mind, heart, and will, I must not resist but go with the Holy Spirit. And when the experience begins to dim, I must return to my ordered meditation.

Distractions and Meditation

A problem which most people encounter in both meditation and prayer is the wandering of the mind. The Eastern approach is to stress the constant and unceasing repetition of the mantra. What advice does the Western approach give?

Distraction in meditation/prayer has its causes most usually in the whole of our lives. It is only when we come to pray that we notice what has been there unnoticed all the time. When we come to pray we do not leave behind the self as we kneel or sit to pray. As the mind and heart are all the day long, so will they be in the presence of God. Having made this observation, we must recognize that the three main causes of distractions are (1) the devil, (2) an undisciplined life, and (3) the psychosomatic unity of human beings (i.e., the interaction of soul and body).

The devil hates to see God's people begin to meditate and pray, and he will do his utmost to assail us with temptations. He must be resisted, but not by violent efforts of mind and will and not by forcing ourselves to ignore the distractions. The right approach is quietly, without anger or impatience, to keep on looking toward God and seeking to rest in the peace he gives and offers. It is to see Jesus before us, saying, "Come unto me." And it is to offer a prayer in words such as "Here I am, Lord.

You know what I am going through. Help me to look to you and so resist the devil's temptations." We commit sin not by being tempted but by falling to temptation. If we go into prayer and meditation with the intent and desire of pleasing God—not gaining blessings for ourselves—then we shall be well placed to resist temptation.

Only the person who is seeking to be holy all day is likely to find that in prayer the door to God actually opens. We can disguise the real state of our hearts before God as we go about our daily duties and activities, but once we begin to pray or try to meditate, then what we truly are becomes evident to ourselves. Throughout the day we need to guard our hearts. St. Peter of Alcántara states that "we must keep our hearts free from all kinds of idle and vain thoughts, from all strange affections and inclinations and from all virulent and passionate emotions" (p. 85). As well as seeking purity of heart, we need to have custody over our senses, those five avenues through which temptation usually presents itself. We can avoid occasions of sin by avoiding many things that are seen and heard (e.g., on TV). Furthermore, we can learn to concentrate in meditation and prayer by practicing concentration in what we do each day. One of the greatest helps to this discipline is to learn to do each thing as it comes as if it were the only thing that we had to do. Thus fully and calmly concentrating on each duty as it presents itself and repressing all impatience and vanity to think of other things, we shall arrive at meditation, intent on concentrating on that duty.

Recollection means being constantly aware that this is God's world, that he loves us, and that we can never escape from his care and presence. We live and move and have our being in the living God, the God and Father of our Lord Jesus Christ. We need to arrange our lives each day so as to provide for ourselves regular reminders that God is always with us and that we live in order to praise and glorify his name. Then as we begin to meditate we are only intensifying what we have been doing all day.

Finally, the third basic cause of distraction in prayer is that we are embodied spirits and enfleshed souls. Illness, tiredness, and stress affect meditation and prayer. We sometimes have to begin by saying, "Lord, I offer to you my fatigue and weariness; may I accept it from you without bitterness but with contentment and so be able to rest in you." By careful ordering of our lives we can avoid some of these problems, but we can never avoid them all; even the choicest saints of God have had to face distraction caused by bodily weakness.

In the Book of Ecclesiasticus (or The Wisdom of Jesus, Son of Sirach), there is a great emphasis upon the value of meditation (6:37; 14:20; 39:7; 50:28). At the beginning of chapter 2 we read,

> My Son, if you aspire to be a servant of the Lord,
>   prepare yourself for testing.
> Set a straight course, be resolute,
>   and do not lose your head in time of disaster.
> Hold fast to him, never desert him,
>   if you would end your days in prosperity.
>
> [vv. 1–3]

Here is sound advice to those who begin the Christian duty of meditating day and night on the Word of the Lord.

Peter of Alcántara: "Meditations for Wednesday and Friday"

St. Peter of Alcántara provided seven meditations for the morning and seven for the evening. The former illustrated the intellectual method, while the latter illustrated the imaginative method. He realized that some people would not do two a day, and so he advised that such people take the exercises over two weeks. They were intended for beginners in order to help them proceed along the purgative way toward the illuminative way.

The topics for the morning included the following considerations: personal sins (Monday), the miseries of human life (Tuesday), death (Wednesday), the last judgment (Thursday), the torments of hell (Friday), the glory of the blessed (Saturday), and all the major divine blessings (Sunday). In all cases the aim is to turn the soul from sin toward the love of God. The topics for the evening were the passion and death of Jesus (Monday through Saturday) and resurrection and ascension into heaven (Sunday).

Peter envisaged that beginners in meditation would stay with these guided meditations for several weeks in order both to progress toward the illuminative way and also to learn the art of meditation in both of its two basic forms. Later they could mix the intellectual and imaginative

125

methods if the topic allowed such a procedure. The meditations for Wednesday morning and Friday evening follow.[1]

Meditation for Wednesday

Thou shalt this day think upon death, which, for the attainment of true wisdom and for the avoidance of sin, is one of the most helpful considerations possible. It aids one, too, in a timely beginning, to prepare for the day of account.

Think, first, then, how uncertain is the coming of that hour in which death is to surprise thee; for thou knowest neither the day, nor the place, nor the condition in which it will take thee. Only thou knowest thou must die; all else is uncertain, save that the hour most often comes when man is least prepared and mindful of it.

Think, secondly, of the separation which must then take place from all those things which we love in this life; and especially of the separation of the soul from the body, its companion of old, and so much loved! If we think banishment from our country, and the air which we first breathed, so great a calamity, even if, when banished, we might take with us all we love; how much worse will be the entire banishment from all household things, from property, friends, father, mother, children, the very light and air we are accustomed to, and all things else!

If the ox when separated from his companion in the plough, sends forth bellowings, what will be the lamentation of thy heart, when they separate thee from all those together with whom thou didst bear the yoke of this life's burdens?

Consider the anxious concern of man as to what awaits the body and the soul after death; how that for his body there is nothing else awaiting than a hole in the ground seven feet long, in company with other dead bodies, and that for his soul he cannot know for certain what is to be

1. G. S. Hollings, ed., *A Golden Treatise of Mental Prayers* (1905; reprint, New York: Morehouse, Gorham; Oxford: A. R. Mowbray, 1940), pp. 21–97.

its lot. This is one of the greatest anxieties we can have
to bear; to know that there is to be for ever, glory or
punishment; that we are so near to one or the other, and
yet do not know into which of these two lots, so widely
different, we have to fall.

Besides this consideration there is another no less serious, namely, the account then to be rendered; a consideration which may make even the stoutest-hearted to
tremble. It is said of Arsenius, that when he was about to
die, he began to tremble. And when his disciples said to
him, "Father, dost even thou fear?" he answered, "My
children, this fear is no new thing to me; it has been ever
present with me."

It must needs be so. For then there will be present
before the man, like a squadron of enemies come to over-
throw him, all the sins of his past life; and those sins in
which he once had most pleasure, will be the sins most
vividly before him, and will cause him the most fear. Oh!
how bitter, then, the memory of past delight which was
once so sweet. Well doth the Wise Man say, "Look not
thou upon the wine when it is red, when it giveth its
colour in the cup, when it moveth itself aright; at the last
it biteth like a serpent, and stingeth like an adder."[2] These
are the intoxications of that poisonous draught which the
enemy presents to us; this is the effect of that Cup of
Babylon, so fair-gilded without!

The wicked man, then seeing himself surrounded by
so many accusers, begins to fear the sentence of this judgment, and to say within himself, "Miserable man that I
am who have lived in such deception, have walked in
such paths, what shall become of me now in this judgment?" If, as S. Paul saith, "Whatsoever man soweth, that
shall he also reap," what shall I, who have sown nothing
but works of the flesh, reap save corruption?

If S. John saith, that in that heavenly city which is all
pure gold, nothing shall enter in which defileth, what can
one look for who has lived so foully and shamefully?

Then, after this, come the Sacraments of Confession,

2. Prov. 23:31–32 (KJV)

Communion, and Extreme Unction, the last succours with
which the Church can aid us in that distress; and, at this
point as at others, thou hast to think what anguish and
distress the man will then suffer who has lived a bad life;
how then he will wish that he had taken another path;
what a different life he would then live, if only time for
it were given him; and how then he would strive to call
upon God—when the pains and grip of infirmity would
give no longer place for it!

Think, too, of those last incidents of infirmity, which
are as messengers of death, how terrible they are, and
what motives to fear; the heaving chest, the fainting voice,
the feet and limbs being numbed, the nostrils and eyes
sinking, the paling face, and the tongue no longer able to
perform its office; and then, last of all, the senses lose
their capacities as the soul goes forth. But above all, it is
the soul which then will suffer most, partly in its disso-
lution from the body, partly in its fear of the account to
be then rendered.

And when the soul is parted from the body, there yet
remain two journeys to make, the one of the body being
borne to its burying-place; and the other, the soul's going
forth to the lot determined for it. When the body has been
left in its burying-place, accompany in thought the soul,
and see it on its way to its new country in which it is to
appear finally for judgment. Imagine thyself present at
this judgment, and the whole Court of Heaven waiting
for the carrying out of its sentence! Then shall be required
the account for the use of life, of goods, of God's inspi-
rations, of opportunities, of means given for true life, and
above all, of the redeeming Blood of Christ! and then
shall each one be judged according to the account rendered by him.

Meditation for Friday

On this day we have to contemplate the Mystery of the
Cross, and to meditate upon the Seven Words then spoken
by our Lord. Awake, then, now, my soul, and think upon
this Mystery of Holy Cross, through the fruit of which is

repaired the loss incurred by the fruit of the forbidden Tree. See, first, how, so soon as the Saviour had come to the place, those enemies set against Him, to make His Death more shameful, stripped Him of His garments, even to the inner "coat," which "was without seam, woven from the top throughout."[3]

Behold, here, with what patience this most innocent Lamb of God suffered Himself to be so stripped, not opening His mouth, nor saying one word against those so treating Him! With goodwill, rather, He was willing to be stripped of His raiment, and to become an open shame, that the nakedness into which we had fallen through sin, might be better covered by His robes than by the leaves of the fig-tree.

Some of our teachers say that, in order to strip off this tunic from our Lord, His enemies with great cruelty tore off from Him the Crown of Thorns which He had upon His Head; and that, after having stripped Him, they replaced it, and thrust the thorns again into the skull, causing the utmost pain. And we may certainly believe that in the course of the Passion they exercised this, as well as many other cruelties upon Him, since the Evangelist especially declares that they did to Him all that they would.

And as the tunic was now fast adhering to the wounds caused by the scourge, the Blood congealed became fastened to the vesture itself; and so pitiless were those savages that in dragging it off with impetuous violence they tore the skin from the Sacred Body, and re-opened all the wounds of the scourges, in such a way that the Body was wholly flayed, and became one great wound from which the Blood flowed in every direction.

Think here, my soul, upon the greatness of the Divine goodness and mercy, which shine forth so brightly in this Mystery. See how He Who spreadeth the heavens with clouds, and the fields with flowers and beauty, is here before you stripped of all clothing! Think of this Holy One in His cold and nakedness and open wounds!

3. John 19:23.

If S. Peter, clad and shod in the Judgment Hall, felt the cold, how much more did He naked and wounded!

Then, too, think of the nailing to the Cross, and of the suffering each nail increased. Well may we think of the Holy Mother in those moments, and feel how the nails piercing those Hands and Feet of her Divine Son were piercing, too, and wounding her own heart also!

Then, when they raised the Cross on high, and fixed it in the socket which they had made for it, letting it fall into its place, think what must have been the pain to that holy Body! O my Saviour and Redeemer, what heart could there be so stony as not to open with grief while thinking of Thy sufferings on that day, when even "the earth did quake, and the rocks were rent," as saith S. Matthew?[4]

O Lord, "the sorrows of death have compassed Thee." "Waves and storms have gone over" Thee. Thou hast been "cast into the deep in the midst of the seas,"[5] and hast found no stay for Thy Feet. Thy Father in heaven hath left Thee alone, what couldst Thou expect from men? Enemies cry out against Thee, friends break Thine heart, Thy "soul is exceeding sorrowful," neither is there any to comfort Thee. Surely my sins were so heavy a weight for Thee to bear, and my penitence should confess it. I see Thee, my King, fastened to a wooden Cross, and Thou hast but three nails of iron to sustain Thee; on them hangs Thy Sacred Body, and it has no other rest. When Thou wouldst support Thy Body upon Thy Feet, their wounds are rent against the nails, which hold them fastened. When Thou dost support it with Thy Hands, the wounds of these, too, are re-opened by the weight of the Body. Thy Sacred Head, tormented and wearied with its Crown of Thorns, what pillow could sustain and ease?

O most holy Virgin Mother, fain wouldst thou have given thine arms to hold Him: but, then, not thine, but the arms of the Cross serve this purpose. Upon them shall the Sacred Head recline, when it would take repose, and the refreshment it shall receive from them shall be the

4. Matt. 27:51.
5. Ps. 116:3; Jonah 2:3.

pressing closer of the thorns! The sorrows of the Son increased with the presence of the Mother; for no less was the heart crucified from within than was the Sacred Body from without. Two Crosses hadst Thou, Blessed Jesus, on that day: one for Thy Body, one for Thy Soul; the one of Thy Passion, the other of Thy Compassion; on the one was Thy Body transfixed with nails of iron, on the other Thy soul with nails of grief. Who could declare, Blessed Jesus, what Thou didst feel, when Thou sawest the anguish of Thy most Holy Mother, whose soul Thou knewest to be crucified with Thee?

After this, thou mayest think upon those Seven Words which the Saviour spoke upon the Cross, "Father, forgive them, for they know not what they do;" "To-day shalt thou be with Me in Paradise;" "Woman, behold thy Son; Son, behold thy Mother;" "I thirst;" "My God, My God, why hast Thou forsaken Me;" "It is finished;" "Father, into Thy Hands, I commend My Spirit."

Observe then, O my soul, with what charity He, in those first words, commended His enemies to the Father: with what mercy, then, He received the robber confessing Him; with what deep feeling He commended the Holy Mother to the beloved disciple; with what burning thirst He longed for men's salvation; with what sorrowful voice He declared His tribulation in the Divine forsaking: then, observe, the perfectly completed obedience to the Father's Will; and, lastly, the commending of His Spirit into the Father's most blessed Hands! Observe, how, in each of those words, there is enshrined the teaching of some special virtue. In the first there is enjoined the duty of charity towards our enemies. In the second, pity for sinners. In the third, pious affection for our parents. In the fourth, desire of the salvation of others. In the fifth, prayer in time of tribulation, when we seem to be without God. In the sixth, the virtue of obedience and perseverance. And in the seventh, complete resignation into the hands of God, which is the summit of all perfection.

Richard Baxter: "The Nature of Heavenly Contemplation"

One of the most widely used textbooks on meditation in seventeenth-century England was Richard Baxter's *The Saints' Everlasting Rest*. I include here part of chapter 13.[1]

1. Once more I entreat thee, Reader, as thou makest conscience of a revealed duty, and darest not willfully resist the Spirit; as thou valuest the high delights of a saint, and the soul-ravishing exercise of heavenly contemplation; that thou diligently study, and speedily and faithfully practise, the following directions. If, by this means, thou dost not find an increase of all thy graces, and dost not grow beyond the stature of common Christians, and art not made more serviceable in thy place, and more precious in the eyes of all discerning persons; if thy soul enjoy not more communion with God, and thy life be not fuller of comfort, and hast it not readier by thee at a dying hour: then cast away these directions, and exclaim against me for ever as a deceiver.

2. The duty which I press upon thee so earnestly, and in the practice of which I am now to direct thee, is, "The set and solemn acting of all the powers of thy soul in

1. Richard Baxter, *The Practical Works of Richard Baxter: Select Treatises* (1863; reprint, Grand Rapids: Baker, 1981), pp. 337–57.

meditation upon thy everlasting rest." More fully to ex-
plain the nature of this duty, I will here illustrate a little
the description itself—then point out the fittest time,
place, and temper of mind, for it.

3. It is not improper to illustrate a little the manner
in which we have described this duty of meditation, or
the considering and contemplating of spiritual things. It
is confessed to be a duty by all, but practically denied by
most. Many that make conscience of other duties, easily
neglect this. . . . As digestion turns food into chyle and
blood, for vigorous health; so meditation turns the truths
received and remembered into warm affection, firm res-
olution, and holy conversation.

4. This meditation is the acting of all the powers of
the soul. It is the work of the living, and not of the dead.
It is a work, of all others the most spiritual and sublime,
and therefore not to be well performed by a heart that is
merely carnal and earthly. They must necessarily have
some relation to heaven, before they can familiarly converse there. I suppose them to be such as have a title to
rest, when I persuade them to rejoice in the meditations
of rest. And supposing thee to be a Christian, I am now
exhorting thee to be an active Christian. And it is the
work of the soul I am setting thee to, for bodily exercise
doth here profit but little. And it must have all the powers
of the soul to distinguish it from the common meditation
of students; for the understanding is not the whole soul;
and therefore cannot do the whole work. As in the body,
the stomach must turn the food into chyle, and prepare
for the liver, the liver and spleen turn it into blood, and
prepare for the heart and brain; so is the soul, the understanding must take in truths, and prepare them for the
will, and that for the affections. . . . It is the mistake of
Christians to think that meditation is only the work of
the understanding and memory; when every school-boy
can do this, or persons that hate the things which they
think on. So that you see there is more to be done than
barely to remember and think on heaven: as some labours not only stir a hand, or a foot, but exercise the
whole body; so doth meditation the whole soul. As the

affections of sinners are set on the world, are turned to idols, and fallen from God, as well as their understanding; so must their affections be reduced to God, as well as the understanding; and as their whole soul was filled with sin before, so the whole must be filled with God now. See David's description of the blessed man, "His delight is in the law of the Lord, and in his law doth he meditate day and night."

5. This meditation is set and solemn. As there is solemn prayer, when we set ourselves wholly to that duty; and ejaculatory prayer, when, in the midst of other business we send up some short request to God: so also there is solemn meditation, when we apply ourselves wholly to that work; and transient meditation, when, in the midst of other business, we have some good thoughts of God in our minds. And, as solemn prayer is either set, in a constant course of duty, or occasional, at an extraordinary season; so also is meditation. . . .

6. This meditation is upon thy everlasting rest. I would not have you cast off your other meditations; but surely as heaven hath the pre-eminence in perfection, it should have it also in our meditation. That which will make us most happy when we possess it, will make us most joyful when we meditate upon it. Other meditations are as numerous as there are lines in the scripture, or creatures in the universe, or particular providences in the government of the world. But this is a walk to Mount Zion; from the kingdoms of this world to the kingdom of saints; from earth to heaven; from time to eternity; it is walking upon sun, moon, and stars, in the garden and paradise of God. It may seem far off; but spirits are quick; whether in the body, or out of the body, their motion is swift.

7. As to the fittest time for this heavenly contemplation, let me only advise, that it be—stated—frequent—and seasonable.

8. Give it a stated time. If thou suit thy time to the advantage of the work, without placing any religion in the time itself, thou hast no need to fear superstition. Stated time is a hedge to duty, and defends it against many temptations to omission. Some have not their time

at command, and therefore cannot see their hours; and many are so poor, that the necessities of their families deny them this freedom: such persons should be watchful to redeem time as much as they can, and take their vacant opportunities as they fall, and especially join meditation and prayer, as much as they can, with the labours of their callings. Yet those that have more time to spare from their wordly necessities, and are masters of their time, I still advise to keep this duty to a stated time. And indeed, if every work of the day had its appointed time, we should be better skilled, both in redeeming time, and in performing duty.

9. Let it be frequent, as well as stated. How often it should be, I cannot determine, because men's circumstances differ. But, in general, scripture requires it to be frequent, when it mentions meditating day and night. For those, therefore, who can conveniently omit other business, I advise, that it be once a day at least. Frequency in heavenly contemplation is particularly important.

10. Frequent society breeds familiarity, and familiarity increases love and delight, and makes us bold in our addresses. The chief end of this duty is, to have acquaintance and fellowship with God; and, therefore, if thou come but seldom to it, thou wilt keep thyself a stranger still; for seldom conversing with God will breed a strangeness between thy soul and him. When a man feels his need of God, and must seek his help in a time of necessity, then it is great encouragement to go to a God we know and are acquainted with. "O!" saith the heavenly Christian, "I know both whither I go, and to whom. I have gone this way many a time before now. It is the same God that I daily converse with, and the way has been my daily walk. God knows me well enough, and I have some knowledge of him." On the other side, what a horror and discouragement will it be to the soul, when it is forced to fly to God in straits, to think, "Alas! I know not whither to go. I never went the way before. I have no acquaintance at the court of heaven. My soul knows not that God that I must speak to and I fear he will not know my soul." But especially when we come to die, and must immediately

appear before this God, and expect to enter into his eternal rest, then the difference will plainly appear; then what a joy will it be to think, "I am going to the place that I daily conversed in; to the place from whence I tasted such frequent delights; to that God whom I have met in my meditation so often. My heart hath been at heaven before now, and hath often tasted its reviving sweetness; and if my eyes were so enlightened, and my spirits so refreshed, when I had but a taste, what will it be when I shall feed on it freely?" . . . Therefore I persuade to frequency in this duty. And as it will prevent strangeness between thee and God, so also,

11. It will prevent unskilfulness in the duty itself. How awkwardly do men set their hands to a work they are seldom employed in! Whereas, frequency will habituate thy heart to the work, and make it more easy and delightful. The hill which made thee pant and blow at first going up, thou mayest easily run up, when thou art once accustomed to it.

12. Thou wilt also prevent the loss of that heat and life thou hast obtained. If thou eat but once in two or three days, thou wilt lose thy strength as fast as it comes. If in holy meditation thou get near to Christ, and warm thy heart with the fire of love, and then come but seldom, thy former coldness will soon return; especially as the work is so spiritual, and against the bent of depraved nature. It is true, the intermixing of other duties, especially secret prayer, may do much to the keeping thy heart above; but meditation is the life of most other duties, and the view of heaven is the life of meditation.

13. Choose also the most seasonable time. All things are beautiful and excellent in their season. Unseasonableness may lose the fruit of thy labour, may raise difficulties in the work, and may turn a duty to a sin. The same hour may be seasonable to one, and unseasonable to another. Servants and labourers must take that season which their business can best afford; either while at work, or in travelling, or when they lie awake in the night. Such as can choose what time of the day they will, should observe when they find their spirits most active and fit for

contemplation, and fix upon that as the stated time. I
have always found that the fittest time for myself is in
the evening, from sunsetting to the twilight. I the rather
mention this, because it was the experience of a better
and wiser man; for it is expressly said, "Isaac went out
to meditate in the field at the eventide." The Lord's day
is exceeding seasonable for this exercise. When should we
more seasonably contemplate our rest, than on that day
of rest which typifies it to us? It being a day appropriated
to spiritual duties, methinks we should never exclude this
duty, which is so eminently spiritual. I verily think this
is the chief work of a Christian sabbath, and most agree-
able to the design of its positive institution. What fitter
time to converse with our Lord, than on the Lord's day?
What fitter day to ascend to heaven, than that on which
he arose from earth, and fully triumphed over death and
hell? The fittest temper for a true Christian, is, like John,
to "be in the Spirit on the Lord's day." And what can
bring us to this joy in the Spirit, but the spiritual be-
holding of our approaching glory? . . . Especially you that
are poor, and cannot take time in the week as you desire,
see that you well improve this day: as your bodies rest
from their labours, let your spirits seek after rest from
God.

14. Besides the constant seasonableness of every day,
and particularly every Lord's day, there are also more
peculiar seasons for heavenly contemplation. As for
instance:

15. When God hath more abundantly warmed thy
spirit with fire from above, then thou mayest soar with
greater freedom. A little labour will set thy heart a-going
at such a time as this; whereas, at another time, thou
mayest take pains to little purpose. Observe the gales of
the Spirit, and how the Spirit of Christ doth move thy
spirit. "Without Christ, we can do nothing;" and therefore
let us be doing while he is doing; and be sure not to be
out of the way, nor asleep when he comes. When the
Spirit finds thy heart, like Peter in prison, and in irons,
and smites thee, and says, "Arise up quickly, and follow
me," be sure thou then arise, and follow, and thou shalt

find thy chains fall off, and all doors will open and thou wilt be at heaven before thou art aware.

16. Another peculiar season for this duty is, when thou art in a suffering, distressed, or tempted state. When should we take our cordials, but in time of fainting? When is it more seasonable to walk to heaven, than when we know not in what corner of earth to live with comfort? Or when should our thoughts converse more above, than when they have nothing but grief below? . . . Reader, if thou knowest what a cordial to thy griefs the serious views of glory are, thou wouldst less fear these harmless troubles, and more use that preserving, reviving remedy. "In the multitude of my troubled thoughts within me," saith David, "thy comforts delight my soul." "I reckon," saith Paul, "that the sufferings of this present time are not worthy to be compared with the glory which shall be revealed in us." . . .

17. And another season peculiarly fit for this heavenly duty is, when the messengers of God summon us to die. When should we more frequently sweeten our souls with the believing thoughts of another life, than when we find that this is almost ended? No men have greater need of supporting joys, than dying men; and those joys must be fetched from our eternal joy. As heavenly delights are sweetest, when nothing earthly is joined with them; so the delights of dying Christians are oftentimes the sweetest they ever had. What a prophetic blessing had dying Isaac and Jacob, for their sons! With what a heavenly song, and divine benediction, did Moses conclude his life! What heavenly advice and prayer had the disciples from their Lord, when he was about to leave them! When Paul was ready to be offered up, what heavenly exhortation and advice did he give the Philippians, Timothy, and the elders of Ephesus! How near to heaven was John in Patmos, but a little before his translation thither! It is the general temper of the saints to be then most heavenly when they are nearest heaven. . . .

18. Concerning the fittest place for heavenly contemplation, it is sufficient to say, that the most convenient is some private retirement. Our spirits need every help, and

to be freed from every hinderance in the work. If, in private prayer, Christ directs us to "enter into our closet, and shut the door, that our Father may see us in secret," so should we do this in meditation. How often did Christ himself retire to some mountain, or wilderness, or other solitary place? I give not this advice for occasional meditation, but for that which is set and solemn. Therefore withdraw thyself from all society, even that of godly men, that thou mayst awhile enjoy the society of thy Lord. If a student cannot study in a crowd, who exerciseth only his invention and memory; much less shouldst thou be in a crowd, who art to exercise all the powers of thy soul, and upon an object so far above nature. We are fled so far from superstitious solitude, that we have even cast off the solitude of contemplative devotion. We seldom read of God's appearing by himself, or by his angels, to any of his prophets or saints, in a crowd; but frequently when they were alone. But observe for thyself what place best agrees with thy spirit; within doors or without. Isaac's example, in going out to meditate in the field, will, I am persuaded, best suit with most. Our Lord so much used a solitary garden, that even Judas, when he came to betray him, knew where to find him: and though he took his disciples thither with him, yet he was withdrawn from them for more secret devotions; and though his meditation be not directly named, but only his praying, yet it is very clearly implied; for his soul is first made sorrowful with the bitter meditations on his sufferings and death, and then he poureth it out in prayer. So that Christ had his accustomed place, and consequently accustomed duty; and so must we; he hath a place that is solitary, whither he retireth himself, even from his own disciples, and so must we: his meditations go further than his thoughts, they affect and pierce his heart and soul, and so must ours.

19. I am next to advise thee concerning the preprations of thy heart for this heavenly contemplation. The success of the work much depends on the frame of thy heart. When man's heart had nothing in it to grieve the Spirit, it was then the delightful habitation of his Maker.

God did not quit his residence there, till man expelled him by unworthy provocations. There was no shyness or reserve till the heart grew sinful, and too loathesome a dungeon for God to delight in. And was this soul reduced to its former innocency, God would quickly return to his former habitation; yea, so far as it is renewed and repaired by the Spirit, and purged from its lusts, and beautified with his image, the Lord will yet acknowledge it as his own; Christ will manifest himself unto it, and the Spirit will take it for his temple and residence. So far as the heart is qualified for conversing with God, so far it usually enjoys him. Therefore, "with all diligence keep thy heart, for out of it are the issues of life." More particularly,

20. Get thy heart as clear from the world as thou canst. Wholly lay by the thoughts of thy business, troubles, enjoyments, and every thing that may take up any room in thy soul. Get it as empty as thou possibly canst, that it may be the more capable of being filled with God. If thou couldst perform some outward duty with a piece of thy heart, while the other is absent, yet this duty, above all, I am sure thou canst not. When thou shalt go into the mount of contemplation, thou wilt be like the covetous man at the heap of gold, who, when he might take as much as he could, lamented that he was able to carry no more: so thou wilt find so much of God and glory as thy narrow heart is able to contain, and almost nothing to hinder thy full possession, but the incapacity of thy own spirit. Then thou wilt think, "O that this understanding, and these affections, could contain more! It is more my unfitness than anything else, that even this place is not my heaven. God is in this place, and I know it not. This mount is full of chariots of fire; but mine eyes are shut, and I cannot see them. O the words of love Christ hath to speak, and wonders of love he hath to show, but I cannot bear them yet? Heaven is ready for me, but my heart is unready for heaven." Therefore, Reader, seeing thy enjoyment of God in this contemplation much depends on the capacity and disposition of thy heart, seek him here, if ever, with all thy soul. Thrust not Christ into

the stable and the manger, as if thou hadst better guests for the chief rooms.

21. Be sure to set upon this work with the greatest solemnity of heart and mind. There is no trifling in holy things. "God will be sanctified in them that come nigh him." These spiritual, excellent, soul-raising duties, are, if well used, most profitable; but, when used unfaithfully, most dangerous. Labour, therefore, to have the deepest apprehensions of the presence of God, and his incomprehensible greatness.

In the next chapter Baxter deals more specifically with the method of meditation—the use of consideration, raising the affections, soliloquies, and prayer.